Enjoy —
Jeanne O'Neill
Riga Winthrop

FORT CONNAH

FT. CONNAH
FACING EAST
DW. LADD 2002

A Page In Montana's History

By Jeanne O'Neill and Riga Winthrop

ILLUSTRATIONS BY DIANN LADD AND JEAN CLARY

FORT CONNAH

◆ ◆ ◆

A Page In Montana's History

By Jeanne O'Neill and Riga Winthrop

ISBN 1-931291-17-9 (softcover)
ISBN 1-931291-18-7 (hardcover)

Library of Congress Card Number 2002109628

First Edition

Copyright 2002 by Dale A. Burk

Published in the United States of America

STONEYDALE PRESS PUBLISHING COMPANY
523 Main Street • P.O. Box 188
Stevensville, Montana 59870
Phone: 406-777-2729

DEDICATION

For George Knapp, who conceived the idea for a book which would recognize the importance and contribution of Fort Connah and the McDonald family to Montana history, and who worked patiently and persistently to see it to completion.

ACKNOWLEDGMENTS

•George Knapp, who suggested this book and who provided materials, time, encouragement and support

•Dale Burk, our publisher for his patience, professionalism, and support

•Joe McDonald, president of Salish-Kootenai College for interviews.

•Laurie McDonald, for information and field trips

•Eileen Decker, who spent a whole afternoon sharing her home, answering questions and telling stories.

•Maggie Good for a telephone interview.

•Rod Wamsley and Kim Sprow for a guided tour of the Ninepipe Museum

•The librarians at North Valley Library, Stevensville, Missoula Public Library, Mansfield Library, Missoula

•Archivists at the Hudson's Bay Archives, Manitoba, Canada

•Vern "Bud" Cheff Jr. and Laurel Cheff at the Ninepipes Museum

•Jennifer Rusk and Chris Sloan at the K. Ross Toole Archives, Mansfield Library, University of Montana

•Our families for patience and encouragement especially, John, Jodi, Jack , and to Joan for technical support.

PREFACE

For those of us that love the history of western Montana, this is an exciting book. It reflects thorough research of the history of Fort Connah. As a boy growing up in the Thirties (1930's), on a small ranch at the site of Fort Connah, I heard story after story about Angus "The Fur Trader" and his wife Catherine. Their graves were down the field from our house and we spent much time reminiscing what it must have been like and wishing we could have been there with them.

I was about ten years old when my grandfather, Joe, a middle son, passed on. My grandfather's brother Angus lived across the field on the other side of the trading post. He died about the same time. Angus would ride his horse up to my grandfather's house. When I saw him coming I would race to the house and sit in the living room listening to them talk. After awhile, they would both go to sleep and I would wander off to play.

I often wish now that I would have had the presence of mind to ask them a thousand questions about their lives that go unanswered now. A few years ago my wife, Sherri, and I traveled to the Highlands of Scotland to visit the area where Angus grew up and to feel what it must have been like to be living there in the early 1800's.

Angus was a strong and robust man. His wife Catherine was equally as strong and self-sufficient. Together they raised eleven children. The most well-known is their son Duncan. I got to know three of them as a young boy. The ones I knew were Angus Colvin, Joe and Tom. They all resided near the trading post.

I barely remember Duncan. He lived at Dixon.

I am delighted that Riga Winthrop and Jeanne O'Neill have written this book. It is an invaluable contribution to the history of Fort Connah and of Angus McDonald.

The Fort Connah Restoration Society did much work thirty years ago to preserve the main structure that still stands on the original site. It is probably the oldest standing building in Montana. The Restoration Society has acquired acreage around it and highway access. They have wonderful plans for Fort Connah that will benefit our posterity forever.

The legend of Angus, Catherine, and the early fur trade in western Montana, northern Idaho, and eastern Idaho becomes real in this book. It put historical fact to legend and I have deep gratitude to the authors for this work.

Dr. Joe McDonald
President, Salish Kootenai College
Pablo, Montana
April 18, 2002

Fort Connah, Hudson's Bay Trading Post, Montana Territory, as depicted in a watercolor painting by Peter Tofft in 1865. Courtesy Museum of Fine Arts, Boston.

This hardwood stave barrel marked with the Hudson's Bay Company insignia was actually used in the trade store at Fort Connah. Today it can be seen as part of a display on the fort at the Ninepipes Museum of Early Montana along U.S. Highway 93 south of Ronan and just a few miles north of the Fort Connah site.

TABLE OF CONTENTS

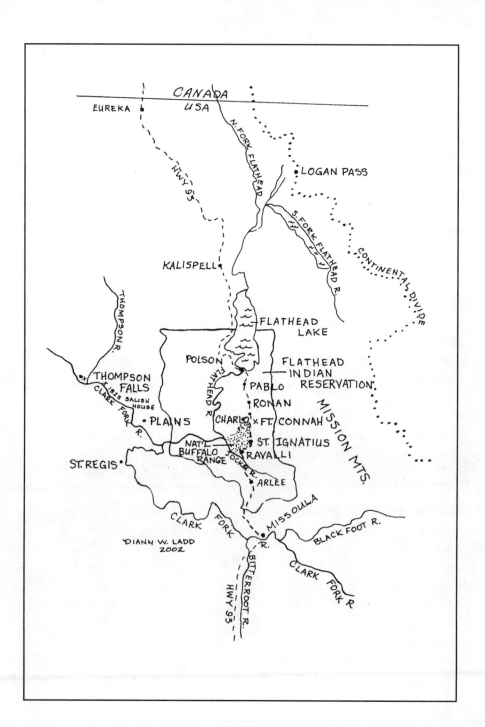

FOREWORD

Most Montanans do not realize that the western third of their state has a significantly different institutional history than the eastern two-thirds. Western Montana was part of the Oregon Country, jointly "occupied" by the United States and Great Britain from 1818 to 1846. Thereafter, it was successively part of Oregon, Washington, Idaho, and Montana Territories. Missoula County, originally part of Spokane County, Washington Territory, was organized and held its first elections in 1860.

Economically, the fur trade dominated the history of western Montana in the first half of the 19th century, and the Hudson's Bay Company dominated the fur trade. Founded in 1670, "The Company" was so pervasive and pre-eminent that its initials, HBC, reputedly stood for "Here Before Christ." The first trading houses in the region were established by HBC employees (or by factors of its rival, the North West Company. The two companies merged – it was a shotgun marriage – in 1821).

One nondescript little building in western Montana holds these two histories, political and economic, together. It is "Fort Connah," located on Post Creek off Highway 93 about halfway between St. Ignatius and Ronan. It astonishes students to learn that Fort Connah – fur trading posts were called "forts;" Fort Connah was never a military installation – was built by the Hudson's Bay company in 1846, Bernard DeVoto's "year of decision," the very year that the Oregon Settlement between the United States and Great Britain extended the 49th parallel to the Strait of Georgia and made western Montana American property. It is even more astonishing to learn from this book that Fort Connah continued in existence for twenty-five years, until 1871 – a foreign business operating on American soil. When Fort Connah opened, "Montana" did not exist; when it closed, Montana Territory, already seven years old, was a boisterous yet prosperous "well-ordered community," in the words of Governor Benjamin Franklin Potts. Fort Connah survived tumultuous times, and its history, so well recounted in the volume you hold, ties together Montana's pre-history and pioneer periods.

You'll find much rewarding information in this book – about the early fur trade, about Angus McDonald and his family, about Native Montanans on the edge of white settlement. Above all, you'll learn about, and be able to visit, a surviving relic of a bygone era, the Hudson's Bay Company's last outpost in the Mission Valley, Fort Connah.

Dr. Harry W. Fritz
Department of History
The University of Montana
Missoula, Montana
April 18, 2002

Book One

FORT CONNAH: ITS STORY

This lone building just north of Post Creek and east of U.S. Highway 93 south of Ronan is the last standing remnant of Fort Connah. This photograph was taken in the late 1960's as efforts got underway to save this part of Montana's historical heritage, and ultimately see it restored. Probably the oldest standing man-made structure in the state of Montana, it was the centerpiece of the Hudson's Bay Company's incursion into this part of North America from 1846 to 1871.

INTRODUCTION

To reach the Mission and Flathead Valley one must travel U.S. Highway 93 which transverses the American Continent from Mexico to Alaska. Five miles west of Missoula, Montana, a large green highway sign along Interstate 90 directs the traveler north to Kalispell, Montana, along Highway 93. Farms, ranches, suburban houses, cabins, and fences are interspersed on both sides of the road which mainly follows a nineteenth century trail probably used for centuries by the native people who lived and hunted here, the Salish (also called Flathead), the Kootenai, Kalispell, Pend d' Oreille, and Nez Perce.

After climbing Evaro hill the road continues north to the Flathead Indian Reservation, to the towns of Arlee and Ravalli, where the National Bison Range is located and where one of the last surviving buffalo herds graze over the hills and meadows. A steep gradient leads onto a ridge which opens up a spectacular view of the valley and the snow-crested peaks of the bordering Rocky Mountains, the Mission Range.

"It seems to me that Montana is a great splash of grandeur. The scale is huge but not overpowering. The land is rich with grass and color, and the mountains are the kind I would create if mountains were ever put on my agenda." (So wrote John Steinbeck in his book *Travels with Charlie,* 1962.) These words could well describe the Mission-Flathead Valley.

These awesome mountain sentinels, which harbor glaciers that feed the streams and rivers which flow into Flathead Lake, overlook the mission church of St. Ignatius and the town that grew around it, a scene as picturesque as a Swiss alpine village. Six miles further north on the east side of the highway a wooden sign directs the traveler to "Fort Connah." A half mile along the remains of a dirt road stands the last outpost of the Hudson's Bay Company in Montana around which flowed the lives of the Indians and whites during the last days of the great fur trade.

At this location, history was made.......

Chapter One

FORT CONNAH
A PAGE IN MONTANA HISTORY

Tucked away in a valley folded into the majestic Mission Range of the Rocky Mountains in northwestern Montana stands an aging and worn log structure, a silent sentinel to a page of Montana history in the era of the fur trade. Fort Connah, 1846-1871, a minor trading post of the Hudson's Bay Company, was established among the friendly and peaceful Kootenai, Pend'Oreille and the Salish Indians, also known as The Flatheads. The British-owned company maintained a network of trading posts across Canada and into the United States with the purpose of trading the Indians for furs, of encouraging settlement and of searching for a water passage from the Atlantic coast to the Pacific. Fort Connah, one of the final western posts, besides being a fur trading post also maintained a commissary line which supplied the other company posts in the western region and became an important link in the Hudson's Bay chain of forts. Because the local Indians hunted deer, elk and buffalo on the great plains east of the Continental Divide, they provided items in constant demand by the Company, such as buffalo robes, heavy coats, and the like, rawhide cords, apishamores (saddle blankets), and hair cords, all of which were necessities in the transportation of the Bay Company's goods on horseback. Also, the Indian hunters brought buffalo and bear, dried buffalo meat, and pemmican for trade. No other post on the west side of the Rocky Mountains could supply these materials in large enough quantities to satisfy the demands of the HBC establishments on the Upper Columbia.

Along with the high adventure of the period, the western thirst for expansion, the struggle for life in the rugged mountain wilderness and the romance of the time, Fort Connah is inexorably tied to the fate and fortunes of the McDonald family, the family of Scots Highlander Angus McDonald

---

BEAVER

This little animal became so important that it was threatened by extinction in the mid 1800's The fashion of "beaver hats" in England and Europe led to a trapping frenzy in America. The beaver had a rich underfur "muffoon" which is microscopically barbed and "felts up" better than any other fur. The felt is natural, without any adhesives or weaving and depends on the matting quality of its fibers. Because of the value of this little animal, free enterprise by traders and trappers resulted in a new and major chapter in American and Canadian history. A continent was explored, a native people's culture and society changed forever.

Beavers are large rodents, (family Castoridae) can weigh up to 100 pounds, have thick furry waterproof coats, powerful web-footed hind legs and small forearms with dextrous sensitive paws. They are the most intelligent rodents, their technical constructive skill, exemplified by their buildings, from logs and mud, dams and lodges (domes up to twenty-three feet in diameters in which they live is surpassed only by that of man). Their powerful incisors fell trees and gnaw logs into shape. Their large heavy tails are used on land for balance and in water for rudder. They can remain under water for up to fifteen minutes. (The New American Encyclopedia)

"Made beaver" are beaver pelts that are cleaned and stretched. They were valued at:

> *In 1800 worth $1.00/lb. in St. Louis*
> *1809 worth $2.00/lb. in St. Louis*
> *1811 worth $4.00/lb. in St. Louis*
> *1812-15 worth $1.50/lb. in St. Louis*
> *1825 worth $3.00/lb. in St. Louis*
> *1834 worth $4.00/lb. at Fort Union*
> *1848 worth $1.00/lb. for large skin at Fort Vancouver*
> *1990's worth $25-35/skin*

By 1850 the beaver fields were trapped out. Silk had replaced beaver as hat of choice and buffalo became the fur of choice. "Days of romantic fur trade are over" (Graves, p. 23)

---

and his Nez Perce wife, Catherine, and their eleven children. Angus, who named the Fort and was the second factor there, remains a most colorful and impressive character among his many descendants as well as on the pages of history which document the period of Fort Connah's existence.

The Indian tribes that inhabited the Flathead-Mission and the Bitterroot Valleys arrived there in the 1600's, and settled in the scenic area at the western side of the Rocky Mountains. Trappers, explorers, traders probably came into the region sometime later but left no written record. However, Meriwether Lewis and William Clark did and made history. On their journey through the Bitterroot Valley the famed Expedition met the Salish (Flathead Indians), who were astonished at these white men, but who greeted them hospitably and perhaps saved their lives. On the return trip in 1806, the Expedition met eleven parties of trappers traveling up the Missouri River *already* on their way to the fur fields and for many on to their destiny. The returning followers of Lewis and Clark told stories of the immense herds of buffalo they saw "they numbered in the thousands", the dense population of beavers slapping their tails all night so no one could get a good night's sleep. and the Indians they met who had never before seen a white man. There for the taking were beaver, otter, mink, weasel, deer, elk, antelope, buffalo. Montana, in the early 1800's, lay open to exploitation of its rich resources. The state's first industry was born – the fur trade.

THE FUR TRADE

The fur trade profoundly influenced the economic life, exploration and diplomacy of the United States and Canada. In the seventeenth century Europe had a scarcity of fur-bearing animals. Consequently, the Dutch , French and English looked to their colonies for fur resources. The New World was resource rich, and also the Indians there were skilled in trapping and processing pelts. Most important was the "profit" factor. Goods that could be purchased in France for one livre, could be traded to the Indians for animal skins worth 200 livre in Paris. Deer, otter, bear, marmot, fox and particularly <u>beaver</u> (for the popular broad-brimmed beaver hats popular in Europe) enjoyed a favorable market in London and on the Continent.

France enjoyed supremacy in the fur trade until challenged by the British Hudson's Bay Company in northeastern Canada which also defied the New York traders in alliance with the Iroquois Indian Confederation. Bitter competition led to the French-Indian wars of 1754-63. The result: Britain wrested control of Canada and all land east of the Mississippi River from France. Fur trapping was an economic boom for markets such as St. Louis, Missouri, but not for the national economy. Exploration of the Rocky Mountains, the Great Basin and the Pacific by the trappers, however, encouraged western-bound settlers who took advantage of the trappers' knowledge of the area. (Groliers Encyclopedia, "fur trade")

For Montana the fur industry was just the beginning of a history of rape and plunder, of a cycle of boom and bust. Montana historian, K. Ross Toole states: "The industry was exploitive and set a pattern for Montana...a century of exploitation. It left little in return for what it took, and it took far more than furs. The influence on the Indian was profound and destructive. Smallpox decimated...liquor debauched the natives, the responsibility being with the companies. The fur trapper and the mountain man knew the Indians more intimately and understood them as well as intermarrying with them and learning their language and customs. Money poured into the coffers of the merchants and financiers. The great Hudson's Bay Company had been enriched, and many an Englishman and Scotsman retired to a country estate to enjoy a leisure based on wealth from the white streams of Montana." (K. Ross Toole, *Montana An Uncommon Land* p. 56-57.)

However, the Hudson's Bay Company and the fur trader are perceived more favorably by historian, Hiram Chittenden. "The relation of the trader to the Indian," Chittenden claims, "was the most natural and congenial of any which the two races have ever sustained toward each other...it enabled him (the Indian) to pursue his natural occupation of hunting...while furnishing him with those simpler articles which directly promoted the comfort of his daily life." (Chittenden, Vol 1, p. 10). Those articles of trade, such as beads, mirrors, tobacco, etc. were valued by the Indians because of their scarcity. Nevertheless, the Indians developed into astute traders. The fur trader knew the Indians, lived with them, intermarried and fought with them against their enemies. Chittenden also notes that the system of monopoly under which the Hudson's Bay Company benefitted the Indian, except when the company was not challenged by competition. Fixed prices stabilized the trade, and the

A trapper-scout in the traditional garb of the era is seen in this painting by Edgar S. Paxson. Courtesy the Mansfield Library, University of Montana.

exchange was equitable. Consequently, the company and the Indians co-existed peacefully.

Another Montana historian, Paul C. Phillips assessed the effect of the fur trade: "while trapping the remote backlands of the west the trappers provided geographic knowledge which led to the development of the areas, contributed to careless exploitation of nature and to a boom and bust transience wherein the bounty from the trade flowed eastward, a recurrence in Montana history. The traders and trappers were huge publicity agents for the West giving it a romantic setting which still holds." (*Montana's Past...*

p. 80)

Meanwhile, The Hudson's Bay Company, which was chartered and given a monopoly by the British crown in 1670, had moved westward and established a network of trading posts among the Indians across Rupert's Land (Canada) and the upper United States. The HBC was a domineering force with absolute control over its employees, but to its credit it did practice conservation in the harvesting of the animals, ran its organization with British imperial efficiency and traded peacefully with the Indians. That is, until it was challenged by the North West Company, a group of energetic Scots from Montreal who started their own company in 1793 and seven years later had 4,000 Nor'Westers trappers and traders in the field. Competition arose which escalated into a war of treachery and violence with no holds barred. The British government intervened and in 1821 the two companies merged under the Hudson's Bay name.

HUDSON'S BAY COMPANY

"The Company", as it is known, is a major fur-trading company and one of Canada's chief business firms dealing in metals, ores, oil, gas, timber and mercantiles. Established in 1680 by a royal charter and monopoly from Charles II of England the company's purpose was to trade in furs in the Hudson Bay Region, colonize, and seek the fabled Northwest Passage. For two centuries the Hudson's Bay Company traded with the Indians, established a network of posts across the wilderness to the Pacific coast, and opened up the region of Canada.

However, before 1670 two French *couveurs de bois*, Medard Chouart, Sieur des Grossaillers and Pierre-Espirit Radisson, working in the Hudson Bay region developed a safer route of transporting furs out of the Indian country in the Lake Superior Region via Hudson Bay and by-passing Quebec. Unable to interest their own French government in their scheme, the two traders turned to Prince Rupert, cousin to the English King, to use his influence with the king and the court. Eventually the Hudson's Bay Company received the charter and a monopoly to "all lands drained by the rivers that entered Hudson Bay", including Montana. Based in London, but with North American offices in Montreal, the Company exercised absolute proprietorship and supreme jurisdiction, both civil and military over its lands. The leaders had virtual power of life and death over its employees and the people within its domain, the first to create maps and records, the first to exploit the potential commercial value of the region. (Graves p. 13-15)

American historian, Bernard de Voto states:

"As long as the Hudson's Bay Company held a monopoly it enforced the wisest of systems:

– conserved the fur crop, practicing conservation and taking only a calculated percentage of the animal population and letting it lie fallow until the population was restored.

–stabilized the market with a fixed price for furs

–developed a heirarchy of organization and command but preserved a career open to talent.

–enforced military government on its employees and

–rigid control of the Indians by a code of wilderness law and punishment.

The name of the company was "Justice" to the Indians, and HBC men could travel the wilderness safely. HBC's record was orderly, the record of British imperial caste dealing wisely, sternly and profitably with any set of natives unlike the bloody record of the Americans which was one of impromptu war and murder. However, when the HBC was challenged by competition it exhausted the fur crop as rapidly as any other. HBC neither gave, traded nor sold liquor until competition invaded its preserves, then HBC had more and cheaper liquor than anyone else ... Final competition with the North West Company meant many years of theft, hijacking, ambush and solitary murder more deliberate than anything the American companies ever saw. In 1821 His Majesty's Government stepped in and forced peace and amalgamation with the two companies."(DeVoto, *Course of Empire*, p. 213-214)

From 1821to 1871 the Company experienced its best years,

especially in the Columbia Region under such outstanding men as Dr. John McLaughlin, Sir George Simpson and Peter Skene Ogden. In 1857 objections were raised to the Company's monopoly resulting in a Parliamentary investigation. This was the beginning of the end of the Hudson's Bay Company's monopoly, and in 1869 a British-United States commission settled the claims of the HBC property loss. The HBC closed its posts in United States territories.

The Hudson's Bay Company maintained a presence in the Flathead-Mission Valley as early as 1810 when Joseph Howse established Howse House, a small fur fort on the northern shore of Flathead Lake which was abandoned in 1811. Trading posts were built and closed in the area, but the noted British explorer, David Thompson built a permanent trading fort, Seelish or Salish House for the North West Company in November 1809 on the Clark Fork River near present-day Thompson Falls. When the Hudson's Bay Company and North West Company merged in 1821 the new company erected a new post on the Clark Fork River upriver from Salish House; it was known as Flathead Post. This was the main HBC trading post in the region which included the Flathead Valley. The Hudson's Bay Company established its Columbia Department headquarters on the Columbia River at Fort Vancouver (Washington) in 1824.

Although the original Hudson's Bay Company traded furs with the Indians, the brigade system, used by the Nor Westerners was adopted after the 1821 merger. The brigade method equipped a strong body of men, horses, and sometimes women and children. These brigades, sometimes numbering over one-hundred, trappers, Indians, family members set out trapping and trading over the better part of a year while surviving attacks from the Blackfeet, severe freakish weather, and adventures that became part of the lore of western history. The number of animal pelts grew steadily until 1837 when one source listed HBC's harvest at 26, 735 pelts. (Graves, p. 21).

American fur companies were also extending their activities into the wilderness which was western Montana, and it was noted that "In 1828 David Jackson and Thomas Fitzpatrick of the Rocky Mountain Fur Co trapped the Flathead region of northwest Montana. They found the Hudson's Bay Company entrenched in the area, which helped neither their spirits nor their trapping. Hudson's Bay reports even made mention that the Americans had to trade some of their small cache of furs to them for necessary supplies. "Pickin's were slim." (Graves, p. 38.)

NORTH WEST FUR COMPANY

An enterprising and energetic group of Scotsmen in Montreal formed the North West Company in 1793. They were innovative compared to the conservatism of the Hudson's Bay Company which they soon challenged. By 1800, four thousand traders and trappers were in the field and eventually controlled the fur trade from the Great Lakes to the Pacific. David Thompson, who is now recognized as one of the world's greatest practical geographers for his map of western North America, left HBC to become a Nor'wester (the name given to the employees of North West Company). He explored around the Kootenai River in Northwest Montana and in the vicinity of Libby, Troy and Lake Koocanusa. In 1808 Thompson built Kullyspell House on the eastern shore of Lake Pend 'd Oreille and Saleesh House, which was the predecessor to Flathead Post near present day Thompson Falls,. Montana. This community is named for David Thompson.

The Pemmican War between the North West Company and the Hudson's Bay Company over the prime fur-territories turned violent when the Nor'westers believed that the Hudson Bay's Red River Colony near Lake Winnipeg, Manitoba, was attempting to interfere with communication with Montreal. When the Nor'westers failed to persuade the governor and the colonists to leave, violence broke out and erupted into a massacre. The British Government intervened and in 1821 the two companies merged under the Hudson's Bay name, although the Nor'westers retained dominance.

The Americans were not to be discouraged, however, and continued their encroachment on HBC territory. In response to the aggressive Americans "Vigorous measures" were taken by the HBC. In 1846 Neil McLean McArthur, who was in charge of Flathead Post, received orders from his superiors in the Columbia Region Headquarters to replace Flathead

Post with another to be constructed in the Flathead Valley in what is now western Montana and was then Oregon Territory. The original Flathead Post was then abandoned but the name was carried on in the company's list as applied to its successor. (Partoll, *Angus McDonald,* p.140) By then the fur trade was in decline for two reasons. The beaver had been trapped out, and the popularity of the beaver hat was being replaced by a fashion trend toward silk. Also, in 1846 the Oregon Treaty extended the boundary of the United States and Canada to Puget Sound along the 49th parallel, giving the disputed Oregon Territory to the United States. The new Fort Connah, flying the flag of the great British fur-trading company, would remain in foreign territory for the next twenty-five years. However, the new post was

---

PEMMICAN AND JERKY

The word "pemmican" comes from two Cree words "pimii" meaning fat, tallow or grease, and "kaan," which means prepared. Pemmican, used by Plains tribes long before white explorers came, was first found useful by Peter Pond, a North West Company trapper.

David Thompson gave out this recipe at Salish House about 1810. "It is made of the lean and flesh parts of the bison, dried, smoked and pounded fine, called "beat meat." The fat of the bison is of two qualities, called hard and soft. Soft is from the inside of the animal, which when melted is called hard fat (properly grease), the latter is made from the large flakes of fat that lie on each side of the back bone, covering the ribs, which is readily separated, and when carefully melted resembles butter in softness and sweetness.

"Pemmican is made up in bags of ninety pounds weight, made of the parchment hide of the bison with the hair on. The proportion of pemmican when best made for keeping is twenty pounds of soft and the same of hard fat, slowly melted together, and at low warmth poured on fifty pounds of Beat Meat; well mixed together, and closely packed in a bag of thirty inches in length, by near twenty inches in breadth, and about four inches in thickness which makes them flat, the best shape for stowage and carriage," Sometimes it was seasoned with wild cherry, wild mint or chokeberries, pounded fine, stone and all. (Graves, p. 20)

not listed in the HBC property for which compensation was to be given according to the Treaty. It was neither completed nor occupied when the treaty was adopted. (Partoll, Ft. Connah, p. 402.)

So, why build a new post? "The Company", known for its astute managers and imperial style was rarely out-guessed. Knowing that it would be forced to leave United States territory, the objective of the British company in moving Flathead Post could well have been to exploit as much of the American frontier before it was forced to leave, (paper from Ft. Connah Restoration Society.) The Flathead Valley, being on the fringe of the trapping area and near to bison country, still had a reasonable amount of animals, but of primary importance were the supplies and goods from this region which HBC depended upon to supply its other posts in the Columbia River region.

McArthur began building the post in 1846 at a site in the valley known to the Indians as *sin-ya-le-min* or meaning "the surround" probably referring to the surrounding Mission Range of the Rocky Mountains. Duncan McDonald, son of Angus, described the location of the post as being "on the open ground above Post (Creek) rather than on the creek's bank , where water, always an important consideration would have been more readily to hand." Duncan also related that a local chief advised not to build along the creek which was covered with brush, for then it would be easy for the Blackfeet to hide and shoot and kill the post's inhabitants. The chief further advised Angus to select a site beside a convenient spring on a gently rising slope a little to the west. The post was built here." (Hunter, p,p. 130 {Duncan McDonald paper, D McDonald to C.N. Kessler, copy letter dated 1918}. The stream near which the post was built was called *in-quith-net-que* by the Indians and was named Crow and Post Creek by the whites. (Weisel,n. p. xxxiii) and is sometimes referred to as Prairie Creek. McArthur left the new post in 1847 because of troubles with the Indians, according to historian Paul Phillips. He become an independent trader at Hellgate. Angus McDonald replaced McArthur with instructions to complete the new post.

When Angus McDonald arrived from his homeland, Scotland, in

1838 he became an employee of the Hudson's Bay Company as an apprentice clerk and eventually traveled to Fort Colville Post (in present-day Washington State). Angus proved a reliable employee and a good manager and in 1842 he was advanced to Fort Hall Post where he met and married Catherine, a Nez Perce woman. Five years later he and Catherine moved with their two children, two-year old John and infant Cristina, to the Flathead Valley. Angus proceeded to build the new post, named Flathead Post in the HBC records, and which would be the last one built by the HBC in United States Territory. The Mission mountains reminded Angus of the home he left in Scotland, and he renamed the new post " Fort Connen" after a river familiar to him in Scotland. However, a local trader, Francois Finlay, had difficulty pronouncing " Connen", probably with a Scottish burr, and Connen slipped into "Connah". Duncan (1849) and Donald McDonald (1851) were born there, making Fort Connah not only a trading post but a family home. At Fort Connah the McDonald home was open to Catherine's Nez Perce relatives as well as to the local Indians who frequently camped near the post as evidenced by infra-red recordings of Indian tepee rings there. The tepees, or mobile homes, were warmer in winter, cooler in summer. The Indians, in families and in bands, roamed freely. The whole country was still their home, and no restrictions were put upon them. No fences encumbered their freedom, the grass had not yet seen a plow, and the region supplied them with game and fish. Angus' rapport with and genuine likeness for the Indian peoples, his position as a family man, and the hospitality shown by the little family at the fort served him well in his dealings with the Indian trappers and the people who visited there. Also, Finan McDonald, subordinate to David Thompson, whose exploits were well known in the region, was a distant relative to Angus, and the father of Helen Grant, mixed-blood wife of the Bourgeois Richard Grant at Fort Hall. Angus never met Finan but Richard's grandfather, also a Scottish Highlander, had settled in the Flathead country (Grant Creek is named for him). These connections probably helped facilitate the good relations Angus always maintained with the Flathead people. (Hunter, p.128-129).

Thomas Adams, an artist with Governor Isaac Steven's negotiating

HUDSON BAY BLANKETS

The Hudson's Bay blankets known as "point blankets" were made in England of warm soft, strong, water-resistant durable wool from England, Wales, New Zealand, and India. They were also colorful which appealed to the Indians, were excellent camouflage, could be made into a capote in winter. A "3 point" blanket was woven with wide colored bands across each end. Colors available: green, light blue, indigo, scarlet. The chiefs blankets were white with stripes, indigo, yellow, red, green.

The indigo blue stripes on the side indicated the "points" or value of the blanket. A full point measured 5 ½ inches, a half point = half of that. Points ranged one to six.

HBC unit of exchange was "made beaver," a term for stretched and cured pelts. A "3 point blanket" was exchanged for three "made beaver.". The colors of the stripes on the HBC "point" blanket coats worn by the French-Canadian voyageurs indicated from where they came. Plains Indians often wore HBC blankets instead of buffalo robes.

In the War of 1812 British Captain Charles Roberts was unable to obtain greatcoats for his men and had coats made from point blankets. The troops captured Mackinaw – and gave the name to the coats. (Graves, p.16 and Hudson Bay's Website) These blankets can still be purchased from The Bay Company for about two to three hundred dollars.

party on the Hell Gate Treaty in 1855 described Fort Connah as:

"A wooden building about 24x16 feet, one story with a bark roof; one wooden bastion about 14 ft. square, and two storerooms each 10 ft. square, also a log corral about 60 ft. square."

The single story building was the family home; the bastion, probably a typical military-type structure made of heavy logs in which there had been cut narrow slits from which a defending party could fire on any besieging Indians. The storerooms were more significant, one of these a warehouse, the other a trading house where Angus would have conducted business with the many Indians who came to trade furs and other commodities. (Hunter, p.131–{Decker papers, 'Duncan McDonald describes the Trading Posts," extract from *Ronan Pioneer,* 11 September 1925.}) Fort Connah was strictly a trading post, never a military establishment.

Angus pictorialized the site, many years later, "...my home fronting the precipitous ridge of *Coul hi cat* now known by the tamer name of Mission Ridge.... the western of the three great bars of the Rocky Mountains, forms the eastern boundary of the Flathead Reservation, and in its sublime grandeur overlooks one of the most beautiful valleys of America." (McDonald: A Few Items of the West, p.190)

So what did the Indian people want in return for their furs and other commodities? Number One: guns. The Blackfeet, their traditional enemy, had long been supplied with guns and ammunition by the British and held an advantage over the Mission Valley Indians who many times were at their mercy.

A listing of other trade items includes:
steel traps, axes, knives, beads, hand mirrors, copper kettle, tomahawks, tobacco, sugar, coffee, HBC tea, strike-a-lights, powder and ball, cloth

Beaver
Jean Clary

blankets (especially Hudson's Bay.)

What about liquor? "Liquor is the most powerful weapon which the traders could employ in their struggles with one another." (Hiram Martin Chittenden.) The Hudson's Bay Company had a policy of not trading

---

FRONTIER FINANCE

Trappers coming into the various trading posts to sell their furs were of many nationalities, some literate, some not. They, as well as the Indians, were puzzled by dollars and cents, English pounds sterling and pence, French francs and fractions, thereof, and Spanish pesos. A system of barter and exchange was gradually developed for the value of the beaver pelt. An example: A gun worth fifty dollars meant confusion, but a gun worth twenty pelts meant something.

A beaver pelt was prepared by stretching and drying it in a hoop generally shaped from a tree branch. This was called "made beaver" which became the currency of the trade in the upper Missouri and upper Columbia River territories including early Montana. In the 1820's-1830's beaver pelt became the standard of value as applied by the Hudson's Bay Company.

prime mink might equal: one "made beaver"

martin or sable might equal : two made beaver

weasel or ermine might equal: eight to ten "made beaver

muscrat: the same

Trade goods:

for 5 beaver = l axe

for 1 beaver =1# gunpowder

for l beaver = 1 knife

for 4 beaver = 1 steel trap

1/4 beaver   = a string of beads

for 1 beaver = 1 hand mirror

down to 1/8 "made beaver" as smaller denominations were recognized. Beaver and "made beaver" became the monetary system on the Montana frontier and legal tender in Montana. Consequently, the frontier fur-trader was among the pioneer bankers of the state who blazed the trail of commerce and enriched Montana's heritage. (Partoll, Legal Tender in Montana) liquor; however, if another company traded liquor the HBC would compete with more and cheaper liquor, a fierce and unrelenting competitor.

Trade at Fort Connah was always done in barter unless currency was the only alternative, usually not true with the Indians. The Company attempted to keep a good stock of supplies on hand for the Indians to assure their continued trade, but credit was not extended.

Twice a year pack trains left Fort Connah with furs and goods destined for the HBC trading post at Fort Colville where boats would be loaded and sent to the Pacific Coast or to other Bay Company depots to north of "medicine line", the Indian name for the boundary between U.S. and Canada. In the spring returns from the different outposts were received and supplies, provisions and goods for the summer trade were sent back. In autumn the pack train returned to meet the fall brigade from the maritime depot, then picked up material for the winter trade. (Hunter, p. 131) Supplies and merchandise were for the most part brought inland from Fort Vancouver on the Columbia River...a lengthy trip past forts Walla Walla, Okanogan, and Colville to a point known as Boat Encampment, where the

Fort Colville, the Hudson's Bay Trading Post in Washington Territory. Courtesy the K. Ross Toole Archives, University of Montana.

Hudson's Bay Company people left boats and crossed the mountains on foot or horseback. Merchandise was generally packed in bundles weighing about ninety pounds for ease in handling. Furs and traded items were brought from Fort Connah by retracing the same route. From 1856 to 1858 Indian troubles disrupted navigation of the Columbia and furs had to be taken overland to Fort Hope in Canada...then to Fort Victoria. Accounts and record books for the post were kept at Fort Colville. (Chief Factor Dugald MacTavish, 1866. Partoll, Ft. Connah, p. 408) "Duncan McDonald, son of Angus, stated that Fort Connah bought about 5,000 beaver each year besides otter, badger, fisher, et." (Weisel, n. p.xxxiv)

In 1846 the United States and Canada signed the Oregon Treaty establishing the boundary at the 49th parallel. The disputed territory now known as western Montana was part of Oregon Territory of the United States. Fort Connah was on foreign terrain from its existence. In 1850, Dr. Anson Dart, Superintendent for Indian Affairs for the newly established Oregon Territory, challenged the legal existence of Fort Connah stating in effect that the HBC posts were not to operate within Indian territory under penalty according to the Intercourse Act of 1834. Apparently, the HBC traders ignored the order as they had more pressing demands and no one was present to enforce it. Again in 1855, Oregon Territory Governor Isaac Stevens ordered the post closed, but again the order was not enforced. So until 1869, when a join British-American commission settled the claims of HBC property loss, Fort Connah remained in business.

Also in 1850, Fort Connah realized a competitor, Fort Owen in the Bitterroot Valley. The trader, Major John Owen, leased St. Mary's Mission at Stevensville from the Jesuit missionaries who had established the mission to the Lower Flathead Indians in 1841. Neither fort was ever a military facility. The traders at Fort Connah had been on good terms with the missionaries at St. Mary in 1847.

However, in 1850 the Mission was struggling due in part to the depredations by the Blackfeet. Also the missionary priests planned to open another mission. To whom? The Blackfeet? Enemies of the Flatheads! The Indians regarded this action as a betrayal. Furthermore, the trappers and traders in the area were jealous of the influence of the priests in the region and spread rumors about them among the Indians. Montana historian, K. Ross Toole, states, " there is some evidence that trader Angus McDonald was planting seeds of doubt and suspicion in the minds of the Flatheads against the Jesuit priests." (K. Ross Toole, *Montana, An Uncommon Land*, p. 62 also Lucylle Evans, *St. Mary's in the Rocky Mountains)* The mission

Father Anthony Ravalli, S.J. Today a town a few miles south of the Fort Connah site is named for this Jesuit priest, as is Ravalli County in the Bitterroot Valley. Courtesy K. Ross Toole Archives, University of Montana.

closed and Major John Owen leased the mission property and established his trading post, Fort Owen. However, at Fort Owen only furs had exchange value while at Fort Connah the Indians could obtain a fair exchange for the products brought in from the buffalo hunts. Although Owen was a shrewd trading rival, he was also sociable and a lover of literature and became friendly with the traders at Fort Connah. Owen was appointed agent to the Indians on the reservation from 1856-1862, but resigned because of the neglect and erratic service of the government in carrying out its responsibilities to the Indians. (Johnson, p. 302)

Angus McDonald served his company well during his tenure at Fort Connah, and, in 1853 he was promoted to the position of Chief Factor at Fort Colville, the central supply depot for the posts in the Upper Columbia Region, from where he would also be administrator of Fort Connah, which was the post farthest east in the HBC's Columbian Region. His replacement, Michael (sometimes spelled Michel) Ogden, was married to Catherine McDonald's half-sister, Angelina. His mother was Indian, his father was the well-known HBC trader Peter Skene Ogden, for whom the city of Ogden, Utah, is named. In 1825 Peter Ogden wrote of the Flatheads: "The Flatheads are a brave, friendly, generous and hospitable tribe which rates them far above the rude appellation of savages when comparing them with tribes around them. They boast of never injuring the whites and consider it a disgrace to their tribe if they are not treated like brothers while

Major John Owen, founder of Fort Owen at Stevensville in the Bitterroot Valley and later agent and friend of the Flathead Indians. Courtesy K. Ross Toole Archives, University of Montana.

in company with them. Larceny, fornication and adultery are actively punished. Their chiefs are obeyed with a reverence due to their station and rank." (Osburne, *Journal of a Trapper* p.33)

Michael, one of the head traders for HBC in the Columbia Region, was living in a temporary trading camp on Lake Pend 'd Oreille in 1853 when he was assigned to Fort Connah. In 1854, Lieutenant John Mullan, who supervised the construction of Mullan Road from Fort Benton, Montana, to Walla Walla Washington, (1858-1862) bought supplies at Post Creek (Ft. Connah) and remarked that Ogden was factor there. The Hudson's Bay Company closed Fort Hall in 1856 because of troubles with the Indians. Consequently, Michael Ogden received the responsibility of transferring all goods up to Fort Connah. He purchased supplies for the trip from Major Owen, his competitor but also his friend, and when Owen's

Angus McDonald. Courtesy Fort Connah Restoration Society.

pack string was traveling in the direction of Fort Colville in 1858 and 1859, Ogden joined him with the winter furs from Connah.(Weisel, p.104).

Ogden was on a buffalo hunt with the Indians in 1857 and also in winter 1860 with the important and influential Pend 'd Oreille Chief Alexander. There, on the Milk River, located in present-day eastern Montana, Alexander's band was badly defeated in a sneak attack by the Crees and Assiniboins. Ogden described the attack when the chief saw his people massacred and his son horribly mutilated. The exhausted, grief-stricken women walked 400 miles packing their children. When the impoverished band straggled through the Bitterroot Valley, Major Owens ordered a pack train of provisions for the destitute people.

In the early 1860's Angus McLeod, Lachlin McLaurin, James McIver and a Mr. Montgomery were living at Fort Connah. (Weisel) Michel Ogden relinquished his post at Fort Connah and turned to farming in 1861. A serious injury from fall from a horse resulted in his losing his mind, and an unpleasant end.

Change was inevitable in the Mission Valley. In 1854 the Jesuit priests, who had established a mission to the Kalispels on the Pend'd Oreille River, found that location often flooded and snow piled late into the season. Chief Alexander led the priests into the Lower Flathead Valley just six miles south of Fort Connah where they founded St. Ignatius Mission. Soon the forests rang with the sound of axes and falling timber. A chapel, two houses, a carpenter shop and blacksmith shop appeared. A large field came under cultivation and fences sprouted up. The following year over a thousand Indians appeared at the mission planning to make it the site of their home camps. Fort Connah had a neighbor and the edges of the wilderness were fraying.

Other changes disrupted the life of the Indians who traded their furs and commodities at Fort Connah. In 1853-54 Captain Isaac Stevens supervised the exploration for a railroad route to the Pacific. On the map Fort Connah received prominence. Gold was discovered in 1858-64 and the stampede of miners to Montana was on. Settlers were migrating to

Washington and Oregon and the Indians there watched their lands being invaded and they fought back. Disturbances around Fort Colville were such that Angus brought Catherine and their children back to the Flathead Valley where they remained among their Indian friends for a year.

It became imperative that the U.S. Government secure treaties with the Indians. Isaac Stevens, now Governor of Washington Territory which included Idaho and Montana, succeeded in persuading the Columbia region natives to sign away their freedom at Walla Walla in 1854. He then proceeded to Hellgate to pressure the Flathead, Kutenai and Pend 'd Oreille. At Council Groves west of Missoula the Hellgate Treaty was signed in July, 1855. The Indians ceded, relinquished and conveyed to the United States government all their rights and interest in their hereditary land which included most of Montana west of the Rocky Mountains. In return the Indians were granted a place to live carved out of their own homeland which they had occupied for centuries. This was the Flathead Reservation. Thereupon, Fort Connah found itself on the Indian Reservation and was seen as "encroaching on restricted land." Article 10 was inserted into the treaty guaranteeing the Indians protection against any claims that the Hudson's Bay Company might have to the property:

"The treaty guarantees the Indians the undisputed possession of their Reservation as against the claims of the Hudson's Bay Company growing out of their Trading Post on the Prairie River (Post Creek) within the limits of the Reservation. It consists simply of three old and small log

---

THE MISSION AT ST. IGNATIUS

In the Mission Valley St. Ignatius was established by Jesuit Fathers de Smet and Adrian Hoecken. The first mission was initially sited on the present Idaho-Washington border in 1845, but when this location proved unsuitable due to heavy snow and flooding, it was moved in 1854 to its present site, a place known as "Snieleman" (a Salish word meaning rendezvous) about six miles south of Fort Connah. In 1864 four Sisters of Providence of Montreal opened a girls' boarding school and a "hospital" in the convent-school. The present church of St. Ignatius, a National Historic Site was built in 1891.

---

houses. Not over two acres of land has ever been cultivated. An estimate will be submitted of its value in my annual report. Notice will be given to cease trading with the Indians at that Post, and if persisted in the buildings will be torn down and the Traders sent out of the Indian Country" (Partoll, p. 407)

Governor Stevens had no way of enforcing his threats and trading continued with the Indians, who preferred Fort Connah to other posts after long and agreeable association with the Hudson's Bay traders. The effect of the treaty, however, was to encourage the Indians to change their free way of life of hunting and trapping and they were urged to become farmers dependent on agriculture. Consequently, Fort Connah was deprived of many of its customers. "The Indians, now considered wards of the government had lost their right of self-determination and could no longer look to the traders for guidance." (Partoll, p. 407) A similar treaty designed to halt Indian raids was signed by the Blackfeet Nation and the Flathead Confederacy in October of 1855. Montana historian Merrill Burlingame, states "The factor at Fort Connah looked askance at the civilizing activities of the missionaries and farmers and guarded the privacy of the forest as best he could in the interest of the Hudson's Bay Company."

When Michael Ogden relinquished his post at Fort Connah,

St. Ignatius Mission in 1862. Courtesy K. Ross Toole Archives, University of Montana.

A special display on Fort Connah and its history can be seen at the magnificent Ninepipes Museum of Early Montana south of Ronan on U.S. Highway 93 and a few miles to the north of Fort Connah. Courtesy Dale A. Burk.

Lachlan McLaurin became custodian in 1861 and served as clerk until 1865. During that time the Mullan Road, named for and constructed by Lieutenant John Mullan, was built between Fort Benton, Montana, and Walla Walla, Washington, and completed in 1862. At one point the Mullan Road was only forty miles from Fort Connah. Some travelers stopped off to settle in the Bitterroot and Missoula Valleys. The wilderness was being tamed, and Fort Connah and its neighbors became less and less isolated as "progress" changed the lives of the original inhabitants of the valleys.

Napoleon Fitzstubbs took over the post in 1865. A flurry of trade took place at Fort Connah as the discovery of gold in the early Sixties in southern Canada attracted miners and their followers as they passed through the valley on their way north. As a result, the Indian Agent on the Reservation, Charles Hutchins, requested that an American trader be sent to the reservation. He also mentioned that he thought the HBC post would offer little competition. A new agent, A.H. Chapman, decided that Napoleon Fitzstubbs – "Stubbs" as he called him – should be removed. "If said Stubbs has no legal right on this reservation and it meets with your approval, I will proceed to eject him and his good from the same." Nothing ever came of the incident, however, and the traders neither curtailed their activities nor abandoned the property as Partoll states, "the traders relied upon the company for orders and let nothing interfere with their execution. And the company was unwilling to abandon its property until financial compensation would be made." (Partoll, p. 412)

James McKenzie, husband of Cristina McDonald, daughter of Angus and Catherine, replaced Fitzstubbs from 1866 to 1867. During its time Fort Connah had come under the jurisdiction of the Oregon Territory (1848), Washington Territory, (1853), Idaho Territory (1863) and Montana Territory (1864). The little settlement of Hell Gate had moved west to become the forerunner of the city of Missoula, and Fort Connah was listed as being in Missoula County. When Fort Connah was built in 1847 the white population was perhaps fifteen persons for the region. On May 4, 1871, the *Missoula Pioneer* estimated the population of Missoula County at 2,555 persons. (Partoll, *Fort Connah, p.* 415)

The last charge at Fort Connah was Duncan McDonald, son of Angus, who was clerk and custodian from 1867 to 1871. In 1869 a joint British and American commission agreed to settle the claims of the Hudson's Bay Company for property lost by the Treaty of 1846 and in accordance with the Treaty of 1863, which was negotiated for that purpose. In the spring of 1870 HBC Chief Factor Roderick Finlayson inspected the posts in the Colville district and reported:

"The Flathead Post in Montana another outstation from which we

Duncan McDonald, Angus McDonald's son and the last charge at Fort Connah, is shown here with Qui Qui Tsu. Courtesy K. Ross Toole Archives, University of Montana.

received a fair lot of Furs last year (was inspected), and as its immediate abandonment would cause serious loss...arrangements were made to continue its business until the close of the Outfit, when C(hief) T(rader). McDonald in his instructions is directed to close it." (Partoll, p.413)

Accordingly, in 1871 Chief Trader Angus McDonald, in charge of the Colville district, ordered Hudson's Bay Company Flathead Post, also known as Fort Connah, on Post Creek in Montana Territory to be closed down. His son, Duncan McDonald, Clerk, attended to the details. By 1872 the powerful Hudson's Bay Company had withdrawn from Montana and consequently from the United States territory. The little outpost, established when Montana was a wilderness, watched the movement of history from fur-trading to settlement and expansion on the way to statehood. The free-moving, independent hunting and trapping Indians who had traded and socialized within and around its doors were now wards of the United States government and were confined to a reservation learning to farm and to ranch. Fort Connah closed its doors and slumbered on into and through the Twentieth Century.

After his retirement, Angus McDonald, who always held a fond place in his heart for the Mission Valley, returned with his family to Post Creek, bought land and built a family home near the old fort. Angus became a successful rancher, and many of his and Catherine's descendants are still living on the Flathead Reservation bearing witness to the strong influence and respect the "old Highland Trader and his Nez Perce wife" received from their neighbors and associates, the Indian peoples on the Flathead Reservation.

Recently, some McDonald family members, friends and associates interested in history have organized the Fort Connah Restoration Project to restore the old post, tell its story and reopen that page of Montana history to which Fort Connah was witness.

Book Two

THE KEY PLAYERS

This faded old photograph shows Angus McDonald with two of his four daughters, identities not listed. Courtesy Laurie McDonald.

Chapter Two

ANGUS McDONALD

Angus McDonald (1816-1889) was born in Craig, Scotland, near the north shore of Lock Torridon. Today the area is uninhabited and called a scenic wild land. Glencoe, the original and more ancient family home-site has a moody and rugged beauty resembling Montana's Mission Valley where Angus and his own family would ultimately settle and he would become a major figure in the valley's history.

He was tall and wiry. Meeting him for the first time in 1855, Edward Huggins, a young Hudson's Bay Company employee, described him, "I had heard a great deal about 'MacDonald,' and was anxious to see him...He was a rather good looking man, about six feet in height, straight and slim, but wiry and strong. He had a dark complexion, with long jet-black hair, reaching to the shoulders, and a thick long and very black beard and mustache. He wore a dressed deer skin shirt and pants, and had a black silk handkerchief tied loosely around his neck. He had a black piercing eye, and a deep sonorous, rather musical voice, and a slow manner of speaking. He was fond of telling Indian stories and legends, and would sometimes keep an audience spellbound, when walking to and fro in the large Nisqually reception room, telling some blood curdling Indian story, in which he had borne a conspicuous part."

In 1838, Angus joined the Hudson's Bay Company, set sail across the Atlantic soon after, and spent a frozen, bleak winter at York Factory on

Angus McDonald. Courtesy K. Ross Toole Archives, University of Montana.

Hudson Bay in Canada. York Factory was the company's center of action and primary trading nucleus for that region because of its central location. It was called a factory but was really a trading house or post used primarily for trade. One of the company's employees called the barrack-like accommodation, with its warehouses and stores, "a monstrous blot on a swampy spot with a partial view of the frozen sea."

Some accounts suggest Angus left Scotland because he had gotten himself into a scrape with English authorities over poaching one of the King's deer. Whether true or not, young men in Great Britain had, for years, embarked on careers in the Indies. Attracted by the fortunes to be gained in the Indian trade, respectable commercial and trade establishments handed out attractive incentives to young men of honorable families. Taking the offer, many of the young men, instead of venturing to the East or West Indies, went to Canada, contracted as clerks for periods of three to seven years. As clerks, or apprentice clerks, they both learned the trade and the protocol of the company in order to later gain a position with more authority, and of course, more money. Ability and merit led to promotion and in the meantime the company expected a great deal from them.

One of Angus' first stations, if not the first, in the Northwest Territory was Fort Colville, located in what is now the state of Washington. It was one of the largest forts in the Columbia River Drainage and the central supply post for other forts in the region. Today, it is beneath the backwaters of the huge Grand Coulee Dam, and its multipurpose Columbia Basin Project, about eighty miles west of Spokane.

The manager, or 'bourgeois' of the fort, was Archibald McDonald, who was Angus' uncle, or more likely, his great uncle. Men from the Scottish Isles had been entering the fur trade for a half-century and more, so it was common to have generations of the same family in the trade. Names of fathers, sons, brothers, and uncles can be found throughout the company's ledgers.

The site of Fort Colville had been chosen for its fertile soil and terrain, and it was a good choice. The farms were both large and productive. Visitors often commented that its geometric fields and whitewashed buildings were a bright spot on the horizon. Archibald McDonald urged the development of agriculture and stock production in the Northwest, and his efforts led to the founding of the Puget Sound Agricultural Company. Under his oversight two hundred acres were cultivated at Colville. The produce was used for trade and to feed the staff and stock economically. In addition to several whitewashed stucco type lodgings, there were corrals, stables, store houses, gristmill, blacksmith shop, cattle, pigs, horses, mules, fences, farming implements, hay sheds, carts, a gig, a sleigh, sleds…. George McClellan (later, General McClellan, Civil War hero) told Angus that Fort Colville was one of the prettiest spots on the Columbia River. It was valued at ten thousand dollars in 1852. (A fair assessment by The Bay Company's, Chief Factor, Sir George Simpson, to settle Article IV of the Oregon Treaty). Father de Smet, a Jesuit missionary, bought a couple of 'milch' cows there in 1841, plus some wheat and seed potatoes. Driving what might have been the first wagon in western Montana, he took the purchases to his new mission in what is now Stevensville, Montana. The mission came to be known as St. Mary's, and although it is not the original building, nor on its original site, it still stands in Stevensville, maintaining the era's history and commemorating its role as the first established community in the state's past.

Angus' arrival at Fort Colville followed an incident of considerable risk. The recounting, written by Angus, gives insight on his emotional response and management of difficult situations. Additionally, we are able to hear the way he told a story.

With much of the passage from Canada behind them, including the Rockies and the Continental Divide, the group exchanged horses for boats once again. This time they were the Bay Company's Columbia River boats that were made at Fort Colville. The boats were manned by 'voyageurs', the masterful French river men whose families had worked the rivers and streams for almost two hundred years.

As their craft turned into the river's current, Big Michel, the steersman or navigator, told his men "calmly yet sternly to row strong". Their job was to run the rapids, called the Rapides des Morts (Rapids of the Dead), carrying Angus and three English families. Angus will continue the story:

"Straight before us within fifty yards roared and heaved and coiled the very whirls wherein the Wallace party with their priest were swallowed. The families were uneasy at hearing the sound of the messenger of death in those whirlpools, it made the party feel that a minute more would tell their fate. On rowing to the lower edge of the dark eddy from which the Rapides des Morts takes his leap, the crew gave one quick side look ahead. Michel cried 'Hurrah, my men, row strong,' plunging and glancing like a pursuing eagle down the headlong leap we landed right in the throat of death's whirlpool and the boat filled and became helpless. The women screamed and prayed and a powerful Orkney blacksmith attending to the water sat forgetting his duty and prayed and wept in the bottom of the boat. The crew held their oars and seats, silent and passive as death. Michel looked fine, but too much like marble to think he was a thing that breathed. He seemed transfixed as hewn granite in his sublime attitude, awaiting any sign of hope. Young and active I thought of a large kettle, seized it and poured in a short number of seconds a large weight of water out of the boat. The whirlpool being then in heaving up instead of swallowing down I cried 'Michel.' He looked at me as if a thrill of lightening passed through his brain and he said again with aroused confidence, 'row strong.' Every sinew found then and there its use and she was rowed by strange luck to the beach. On landing the whole of the crew and all the families looked with joyful terror on the grim folds of death that streamed in its foam before them. Until this I felt no fear, but now…I felt a rising spasm chocking me. I never felt it before. I drank a good draught of snowy water and walking away my nervous spasm was laid."

In the early 1840's, there is mention of Angus at Fort Simpson (in British Columbia), Fort Nisqually (in Washington, today), and Fort Boise, (now Idaho). However, his station at Fort Hall is the period when he began to distinguish himself in the company. The position of clerk, held by Angus, was one of the most rigorous and demanding positions in the trade, according to historian, Hiram Chittenden. Dangerous travel was required. At appointed times, supplies, equipment and other paraphernalia were packed to Indian villages, and there the traders lodged until the wares were depleted. The newly purchased items were then packed and loaded for the trip home. Bay Company trade supplies and materials were transported by pack-strings. Materials, or stores, were packed into sacks, each weighing ninety pounds; ninety pounds per sack, two sacks per mule or horse.

The duties and responsibilities of the bourgeois fell to the clerk when sickness, travel or other incapacities took away the post's leader. Some of the operations at the fort were: the care and packing of the furs; tending the

Angus McDonald's powderhorn and other period artifacts. Courtesy Eileen Decker.

horses, which had to be watched because of Indian theft; care of the gardens, stock, and inventory; hunting and preparation of meat provisions; and bartering with Indians and trappers. Some of the trappers they traded with were hired servants of the Company, others were free trappers and mountain men, and some lived among the Indians. A few were itinerants who wandered from place to place. Trappers and mountain men often lived alone without amenities or comfort for long periods of time. The weight of isolation, the dread and guard against everything in the field, in addition to regular exposure to scenes of violence and death made them hard-bitten men. Most were decent, but many were desperate, and some of them outlaws who knew the enforcement of codes of justice did not reach into the territories. Angus, other clerks, factors, and bourgeois had interchanges and trade with those impatient and suspicious men, and the exchanges required great skill on their part, in addition to diplomacy and control.

Fort Hall was a station on the Oregon Trail, a great migration route across the plains that was carved by the feet of Indians, wild game, mountain men, trappers, and covered wagons. It was not a surveyed and 'built' road, but an overland trail that covered two thousand miles from Missouri to the fertile Willamette River Valley in Oregon. (The Mormon Trail branched off the overland route and headed for Utah.) The register at Fort Laramie (now Wyoming) in 1850 recorded thirty-nine thousand five hundred six men, and a little over three thousand women and children for that season. It is estimated five hundred thousand people used the trail and its cutoffs. The pioneers, in white, canvas-topped wagons, hauled all of their possessions across the country to take up a new life in a rumored, far-flung Eden. The arduous journey took several months of passage, and traveling along the tough path the emigrants found few places of safety for rest, repairs, or trade. Finding the helpful and friendly hospitality of the traders at Fort Hall motivated one traveler to write about Angus and his bourgeois, Richard Grant: "Both were Scotchmen and gentlemen. They treated our party with great courtesy. They furnished us with a written guide for the journey westward with all the company places specified, the distance from each to the next, with information as to wood, water and grain, which was of exceeding value."

Angus described trade at Fort Hall as "large". The fort was on the southern bank of the Snake River, seventy miles from the present border between Idaho and Utah. (It is now beneath the waters of the American Dam near Pocatello, Idaho.) Indians traveled through the Snake country at least twice a year to hunt buffalo, bulls in the spring and fat cows in the fall. Every able-bodied member of the band traveled to the hunt. The women butchered and dried the meat, the girls took care of the younger children, the older boys were responsible for the extra horses, and the men of course, sought and killed the buffalo. Bands of Indians stopped and camped and traded at the Fort during those expeditions. Trappers came and went in all directions from the fort. The Oregon Trail emigrants traded broken down, foot-sore stock for flour and other supplies, or animals that were fit for travel. It became common practice to trade two worn-out animals for one hardy animal. The post would pasture the ailing, worn-out stock until they were fat and strong, and ready for trade again. The sites where the trading was done were called 'Tenderfoot Stations." That type of trade was a precursor. In a short time period, as more settlers arrived in the territory, it became more profitable for trappers and mountain men to trade with settlers, or miners, than to trap and sell furs. The cattle business was about to spring into life and find its feet quickly. Stock production was to hold a major economic position in the West, along with grain and mining.

Angus gave some consideration to homesteading during that period. In 1844, he wrote to Dr. McLaughlin, Chief Factor of the Hudson's Bay Company, and in command of the Columbia Department, asking permission to leave the Bay Company. McLaughlin was legendary for his leadership and administrative ability. Bernard DeVoto, historian, said, his "ten years as resident king had made the Department of the Columbia as neat as a blueprint". The Indians were impressed by his size, which was well over six feet, and his shock of white hair. They called him, "White Eagle". McLaughlin responded to Angus, saying that he would not release him until another year elapsed. By that time, Angus had received commendation and promotion and no longer thought of leaving the company.

Politics were rife in the 1840's. Who would control Oregon? Britain had first occupancy and Hudson Bay drainage rights, plus their Hudson's Bay Company had land, buildings, property, and virtual control of the Northwest fur trade for well over one hundred years. Was possession nine-tenths of the law? Or, would the U.S. politician's desire for control of the country, all the way to the Pacific Coast, and the settlers increasing demands for control of the land take precedence? Feelings in the country were high. Slogans proclaimed, "America for Americans," "Fifty-four forty or fight."

One of Angus' fellow employees said, Angus "never missed an opportunity of getting into a wordy quarrel…(over the Oregon Treaty of 1846) until I refrained from taking him with me when I visited adjoining towns." The Oregon Treaty established the boundary line between the United States and Canada along the forty-ninth parallel, giving America control of the country below, or south, of the border, and thus the Oregon territory. This left the Bay Company on foreign soil and subject to American jurisdiction. Angus continued upholding his company. A Bay Company worker commented, "Angus periled his life in support of the company….". Respected and spoken of highly among employees of the company, Angus found himself with increased salary and in a position with more authority.

There was another major change in Angus' life during this period; he became a family man. He met and married Catherine, a Nez Perce-Iroquois woman. The couple were married in a civil ceremony at Fort Hall in 1842. The fort's bourgeois, Richard Grant, performed the ceremony.

It is thought Catherine was born in 1815, making the new McDonalds close in age. Members of her family were leaders of the Nez Perce people. Two of them were Eagle of Light and White Bird. Her Mohawk-French father, Baptiste, participated in the War of 1812, taking the British side. He recounted anecdotes of his adventures to Catherine. Angus, over the course of their life together, copied them down in his large ledger. He also transcribed her account of a trapping and trading expedition taken with her father and stepmother to the mouth of the Colorado River.

In 1847, Angus and Catherine, with two young children, left Fort Hall for a new assignment in the Mission Valley. Angus was to be in command of the post. His first job was to complete construction of a newly located fort that his predecessor, Neil McArthur, had begun. When completed, the new post was no longer called Fort Flathead, or Flathead House, but was renamed, by Angus, Fort 'Connen', after a river in Scotland. Connen transformed into Connah, probably for ease of pronunciation by non-Gaelic speakers (See Page 28).

Angus' relationship with the Indians in the valley was friendly and mutually respectful. There were ties to his wife's family, which surely eased exchanges and relations. He frequently joined his in-laws and Indian friends to hunt, and sometime in face-offs with hostile Indians. He felt comfortable enough to participate in a San-ka-ha Ceremony, a farewell to warriors on the eve of battle. During the ceremony, dancers performed to grave, impelling, musical strains as sorrowful women cried. Angus said, "I stripped with the leading men, painted with vermilion the grooves and dimples of my upper body, and mounted on my black buffalo charger with full eagle bonnet, cantered round with them, keeping time with the song".

Edward Huggins, a Bay Company employee, said Angus "could talk several Indian languages." Over the years he learned Salish, Nez Perce, Kootenai, Blackfeet, Okanogan, and Crow, and also spoke Gaelic, English, and French. The ability to communicate in other languages was beneficial commercially, but to understand and speak with Indians on the frontier was also advantageous. Angus had always been fair with the Indians, and most of them respected him. Encounters with them as he traveled through their territory illustrate their regard for him. The Yakima, who had recently killed a government official, and in so doing declared war on whites, allowed

Angus, his men, and their pack-string to pass through their territory without confrontation. The pack train was transporting supplies, which included guns and ammunition, but was allowed to proceed back to Fort Colville from Nisqually without trouble. Telling about this incident in his journal, a Bay Company man reported, "Had any other man but McDonald been in charge of the pack train, the whole outfit would no doubt have been sacrificed and the men murdered, for the goods would have been of great value to the already hostile Indians."

During the time of turbulent Indian uprisings Angus sent Catherine and the children back to the Mission Valley from Fort Colville. If the fort were to be attacked he knew they would have the protection of the Flatheads. Angus' faithfulness to Catherine waffled a bit at that time. Duncan, their son, explained why two other boys in the family are called Angus. "The mother of Angus Pierre put up in the same bed with father when my mother was away for about a year." The other woman was an Okanogan Indian, and according to Duncan, Catherine was kind to the woman and the boy.

In 1854, Angus and Catherine had their marriage solemnized by a Jesuit priest. Angus' religious views, however, remained idiosyncratic. The McDonalds lived out their lives together. They had twelve children, several of whom continued to live in the Mission Valley, and many of their descendants still do today.

Angus had a sound education and a life long appreciation of literature. He wrote poetry, plays, and graced his friends with lengthy correspondence, his writing usually carrying literary and philosophical allusions. He was known to have "a quite respectable library". It included a full set of Shakespeare, some of which he usually carried with him in his travels. Angus enjoyed sharing his interest in books and ideas with others of a similar mind. Surprisingly, one of them was rugged frontiersman and later lawman, Joe Meek, who was legendary for wrestling with an angry sow bear and coming away alive. Major John Owens, Angus' Bitterroot competitor, was another literary devotee who had a sizable library of over three hundred volumes; and an American soldier, stationed near Fort Colville, who must have known Angus' appreciation of words, left all of his books to him when the troop moved on. George Hodges, a free-trader and friend of Angus wrote: "After an evening of quiet discussion (over) a Bottle of fine old Brandy and a fine 2 pipes of tobacco… The following morning I walked about with McD visiting his different Shops barns fur Room etc He has a fine lot of Cattle hogs poultry pigeons etc found a very respectable library and was the recipient of a fine present of 4 vols of the Dictionair Bible with Extension & enlarged Notes handsomely guilt." Angus, and others, are among the many frontiersmen who broke the rough and ready, illiterate stereotype when worn volumes of the Bible, Shakespeare, and classical writers were found in their belongings.

Music was another love. He was fond of singing and often sang and chanted in Gaelic. Hearing the Jews' harp played while he was in Victoria (British Columbia), he said of his own playing, "…the mouth of the initiated makes a very soft and sensitive harmony." His daughter, Christina, noted, "Once when I was with him (Angus) in Victoria he engaged a coach and taking Hugh MacLean, a bagpipe player, we sat off to pay a visit… to an old acquaintance who lived near Esquimalt" (Angus' friend and a former Colville bourgeois, A. Anderson). " Driving to Anderson's the woods rang with MacLean's spirited playing". Angus owned and played a set of bagpipes, frequently playing his instrument at Indian campfires. The Salish were intrigued, and called it his "bag that whistles." Musing about his bagpipes, Angus said, "I believe that on the last day when you hear the sound of the trumpet that you shall hear the sound of the scotch bagpipe as it is longer and louder."

Angus seems to have struck a stance, or attitude, of balance and evenness in his life. He enjoyed and was comfortable with most Indians; recognizing others for their "evil manner and cunning." He took care of his family; supported his children's education by establishing schools; provided musical instruments; and sought out tutors and teachers for them. He spoke fondly and affectionately of his wife in his correspondence. But, he was also comfortable and enjoyed his times in the society of his highly accomplished friends in the sophisticated settings of Victoria and British Columbia. He wrote about teas and conversations with old widows of the Bay Company; dinners he attended with earls and their ladies; and brandy with judges entertaining continental French guests. There were convivial times with governors, magistrates, old pursers and blacksmiths from 'the trade', and his "hospitable" friend who had been knighted by Queen Victoria. While sipping tea, cognac, and wines they enjoyed discussions of politics, both national and international, Indian policies, love scrapes, Gaelic poetry and other matters and ideas of the time.

Angus' colorful life style gave rise to interesting, lively and memorable occasions. Catherine was part French and spoke the language, probably learning it from her father. Angus also spoke French and it was decided, between them, they would speak French to the children at home. As the girls became older they were the "belles of the ball". A young English surveyor wrote, "We had the other day a grand ball up at the Hudson's Bay Fort given by Mr. McDonald... Some of the Canadian boat songs sung by a lot of voyageurs were capital... at four o'clock in the morning, I found myself dancing a reel de deux with an Indian maiden in a state of uncertainty as to whether I had any legs at all, having danced them clean away, and nearly dislocated them in the bargain, by trying to pick up the proper step, a kind of spasmodic kick in which the legs are doubled up and thrown out in the most extraordinary manner." In 1860, the McDonald Christmas table replete with roast beef and plum pudding was appealing and festive for their guests. Following the traditional holiday dinner, Angus performed a sword dance. Never weaned from the Highlands, he called upon hundreds of years of ancient Scottish culture, and danced around two broadswords lying crosswise on the floor.

THE CHIEF TRADER

Angus returned to Fort Colville in 1852 as the post's bourgeois. The bourgeois were men of high ability according to writer, H. Chittenden. They are compared with today's C.E.O.'s or captains of industry because of the administrative skills and strategic abilities needed to perform their job. Some of the duties or job description of the bourgeois were:

•Controlled trade policies with the Indians in the post's geographical area.

•Sent traders (clerks, etc.) to tribes for trade as necessary

•Organized trappers to work designated areas

•Selected hunters for the post

•Directed the scope of gardening or other means of obtaining staple foods for all supervised posts.

•Chose subordinates to trade with Indians.

•Chose subordinates to pack and care for furs.

•Tended the book keeping and correspondence with home office and heads of other supervised stations.

•Travel as necessary.

The fort's customers included some volatile Indians and difficult trappers, a situation demanding shrewdness and finesse to both make a profit and to stay alive.

The position of Chief-Trader was awarded Angus in 1856. Within the Bay Company that was about as high as a field officer could rise. The system of promotion was based on discipline and absolute subordination of individual interest to that of company policies. Employees were frequently switched to other areas to end questionable activities and punish workers. A move was also often used to reward good workers. Those practices protected the company from incompetent workers and held the loyalty and respect of employees of quality.

By 1860 the Hudson's Bay Company's hold on Indian and fur trading was approaching the end of the line. The company's presence south of the forty-ninth parallel was in defiance of the 1846 Treaty. The International Council awarded the Bay Company compensation for its forts, farms and properties in the United States' domain, but the settlement was long outstanding. The company would ultimately receive four hundred fifty thousand dollars for its rights, and two hundred thousand dollars for its holdings of one hundred sixty-seven thousand acres of land (Between the Puyallup and Nisqually Rivers, from Puget Sound to the Cascades). As things stood, it was almost ten years before any payment was issued, and until the settlement was paid, the forts, farms, and all business were to continue as usual.

Meanwhile, settlement, technology and changing land use were transforming the Northwest. The changes affected trade in a much greater way than fashion's fickle trend to silk. Peter Ogden, a famous trader, said that neither the fur trade nor Indian societies were compatible with white settlement. The ecosystems that both groups needed were irreconcilable to the needs of the colony communities. For decades, as settlers continued their push west, fur traders had repeatedly moved to new terrain. Indians, by the 1850's, became desperate in the attempt to hold their territory. Open ranges, which had always supported them, were being destroyed. Ultimately, they were driven to Reservation life.

In 1853, modern technology raised its head in the West. Surveys were made for a Military Highway (later called Mullan Road), and also to establish a route for a rail system from the Mississippi River to the Pacific Ocean. (Or specifically, from St. Paul, Minnesota to Puget Sound, Washington.) One of the survey camps was only about a mile from Fort Colville. Angus, as its bourgeois, was given instructions from Bay Company headquarters to extend hospitality to Isaac Stevens, head of the survey and Governor of the recently organized territory of Washington. Angus willingly complied, inviting both Stevens and Captain George McClellan, a member of the survey team, for an evening at the fort. (McClellan later became a hero and a General in the Civil War.) Catherine prepared a nice meal of buffalo steaks while Angus provided plenty of 'spirits', and enthralled the men with legends and thrilling stories which he enjoyed sharing. Stevens, as Angus noted, " had shown himself fond of it (the brandy)" and after a while made his way to bed. "His last words that night were ' Mac this is powerful wine'." McClellan continued enjoying the evening. Angus remained the cordial host, conversing buoyantly and freely dispensing "spirits", until McClellan quietly slipped down off the sofa to the floor. Later, at Fort Vancouver, Bay Company headquarters, Stevens told them about his "hospitable friend (Angus) who received him as a brother at Fort Colville." McClellan and Angus continued their friendship through correspondence.

THE CLOSING

Finally, in 1869, the United States government paid six hundred fifty thousand dollars in gold bullion to the Hudson's Bay Company, settling the possessory rights issue, and sealing the fate of Fort Connah. The Bay Company would move all operations north of the forty-ninth parallel. There was no longer any defense for remaining in the States.

Robert Newell, a mountain man, summed up the condition of the fur trade in 1869, telling his friend Joe Meek:

"We are done with this life in the mountains,
Done with wading in beaver streams and
Freezing or starving alternately, done with
Indian trading and Indian fighting. The
fur trade is dead in the Rocky Mountains,
and it is no place for us now, if it ever
was....We are young yet and have life
before us. We cannot waste it here."

Angus adapted to the New West with his usual sharpness in practical matters. Before the fort's closing he became a naturalized citizen of the United States, giving him authorization to land claims and other privileges held out to American citizens. Using the provision of squatter's rights,

Angus remained in possession of some of the land surrounding Fort Colville. His sons, Duncan and Donald, and possibly cousin Ranald (Archibald McDonald's son) went into business there. Angus, Catherine, and the younger children returned to the Mission Valley. He sold his share of interest in the Bay Company and obtained a large portion of land in the Post Creek area near Fort Connah. The Flathead's Chief, Victor, welcomed his McDonald friends return to the valley.

The former fur trader became part of the settlement movement in the valley, acquiring land and many head of Galloway and Shorthorn cattle. The increasingly large herd carried on their hip the MD brand. They ranged up and down the unfenced valley, twenty miles or more, and numbered close to two thousand head before Angus died. After his death, they were divided among his family. The old fur trader successfully managed his affairs and became a prosperous rancher and prominent member of the territory. He remained vigorous until a fall hastened his death at his Post Creek home in Mission Valley. The site for his burial place was in the valley, or " glen," he so greatly admired; near the family home he built, and not far from old Fort Connah, which he had completed years before. The inscription on his headstone, which sits behind a wrought iron gate in an old Victorian cemetery, says:

Angus McDonald

Native of Scotland

Born October, 1816 – Died Feb 1, 1889

Perpetuating Angus' memory are some geographical markers:
•McDonald Peak in the Mission Mountains
•McDonald Lake, named for the family, in Glacier National Park.

Angus McDonald's tombstone showing the variant spelling of "MacDonald."

Chapter Three

THE NATIVE PEOPLES

T he native peoples living in the area surrounding Fort Connah

were the Flathead and the Pend d'Oreille, two tribes of the Interior Salish.
The Kootenai lived north of Flathead Lake, and some linguists believe their
language had Salish roots. To the east of the Continental Divide, were the
Blackfeet, traditional enemies of the Salish. The Nez Perce, friendly to the
Salish, lived west of the Bitterroot Mountains into Idaho. Their lands were
richly endowed with fur bearing animals. For well over a century the British
and French had developed trade in furs into a profitable business, and later,
for Americans, it became the first venture capital industry of the West,
followed by gold, cattle, grain, and mining. The fur trade supported many
men. Some of them became rich, and a few claimed great wealth.

The articles acquired in barter from trade in furs provided little
toward the long-range prosperity or welfare for the Indians. Interaction with
whites did bring disease, liquor, devastation, and increasing suspicion and
cynicism toward whites, and ultimately leading to a conviction of their
deceit and dishonesty. Increasing white encroachment and subsequent
Indian attempts to deflect the intrusion created warfare, but as trader Angus
McDonald told an Indian friend, there was no use fighting the white man.
One or two might be killed but they were like ants; more kept coming.

The U.S. government dealt with Indian tribes as they did foreign
nations which owned land and resources. Treaties were delineated and

councils were convened. Through treaty rights and orders, large tracts of land were reserved for Indian tribes. Reservations today are still the cornerstone of Indian life and policy.

THE HELLGATE TREATY

In the summer of 1855 the Governor of the territory of Washington and Superintendent of Indian Affairs, Isaac Stevens, met with the Salish to negotiate a treaty near Missoula at a spot which came to be known as Council Grove. The Flathead, Kootenai, and Pend d'Oreille chiefs, Victor, Michael, and Alexander met with the governor. The Bitterroot Salish did not want to move from their home in the valley. The Kootenai and Pend d'Oreille found the one million two hundred eighty thousand acres of reservation land along and south of Flathead Lake acceptable. However, Victor did not. Stevens, against his inclination, agreed to establish a reservation in the Bitterroot for the Flatheads. Historical author Lucylle Evans states in her book *Good Samaritan of The Northwest*, a biography of Father Anthony Ravalli, S.J., a missionary at St. Mary's in Stevensville, that "Ravalli informed Senator George G. Vest of Missouri that he had been present at (a later) signing of the agreement" and while the other chiefs did sign the document, "Charlot (Victor's son, and hereditary chief of the Flatheads) did not sign it."

The Hellgate Treaty also called for payment of one hundred twenty thousand dollars per year for twenty years. There were several articles attached to the treaty, including: the Indian people were to have aid in agricultural education and equipment, a government supervisor, a system of apprenticeship in trades for young men, and education for young children. There was an added provision stating that at the discretion of the President, an area of land might be assigned to individual Indians as their personal home.

Private ownership of land was a foreign and unappealing concept to Indians whose value system was inclusive. They believed the earth to be sacred and not owned by men. Personal ownership of land would not give them a sense of pride. In 1872 the Bitterroot Valley was opened to white settlement and arrangements made for the Flatheads to be removed to their new Reservation home to the north. However, Chief Charlot and his small band did not leave their ancestral home in the Bitterroot to move north until 1891.

Subsequent passage of the Allotment Act of 1887 meant each member of the tribe could receive ownership of a tract of land and the rest was opened for homesteading; this destroyed the tribe's land base and the character of the reservation. The story of the Hell Gate treaty and subsequent treaties was unchanging and monotonous in its disregard for what had been promised the Native Americans. Contemporary tribal authorities state that much of what was promised never came to be, but that is a story for another time.

Montana today has seven reservations on which about thirty-four thousand Native Americans live. About thirty-five hundred of those live on the Flathead Reservation. The Flatheads are one of the most self-sufficient and prosperous tribes in Montana. Their push for self determination over the past several decades has given them management of most government programs on the reservation. They are actively engaged in the management of their rich natural resources, and have taken legal means to establish their treaty rights and they've articulated a policy of commitment to becoming economically independent and less vulnerable to the Federal government to prevent unnecessary exploitation.

Catherine McDonald.

Chapter Four

CATHERINE McDONALD

Angus McDonald's wife, Catherine, was an attractive, Nez Perce woman. They were married in 1842 by the bourgeois of Fort Hall, Richard Grant, who, at that time, was Angus' superior. Catherine's mother was a Nez Perce whose bloodline had several leaders and chiefs. One of them was Chief Looking Glass, who was one of the major leaders of the Nez Perce in their battle with the United States army in 1877; another was Eagle from the Light, and White Feather, both of whom were leaders during the conflict and played a role. Eagle of the Light was a favorite of Angus, and he said about him: "a most eloquent... old blood. From him I learned many an item about the Nez Perce." Angus, many years later in his marriage, said his mother-in-law was "one of the last old royals of the Nez Perce. She in her age is still fine of face and of decidedly aristocratic speech and conduct."

Baptiste, Catherine's father, married into the Nez Perce tribe. His mother was Mohawk, and his father was French. Baptiste came to the Northwest from the northeastern region of the United States, urged by the fur trade, as other Iroquois had been. They hoped to engage in the trade as canoe-men, guides, interpreters, hunters, or trappers. The Iroquois were a six-tribe (or nation) confederacy to which the Mohawk belonged. (The others were the Seneca, Onondaga, Oneida, Cayuga, and Tuscarora.) They were skilled at managing canoes in rapids and hazardous waterways, and were accomplished trackers, hunters, and beaver trappers.

There is speculation that Catherine and Angus met during the outfitting of a trapping and trading expeditions in which she and her father, stepmother, and their two children were to take part. It was to be a large expedition. The party numbered one hundred eighty men or more, in addition to women and children who were not counted.

Catherine, like most Indian mothers, told her children stories and legends to provide entertainment and pass on information. Indians are a people of oral tradition, and like so many women before her, Catherine had internalized serial stories and legends for needed occasions, especially long winter days and nights. Her personal adventure story of the experiences encountered with her father on the 1841 trading expedition was one she shared with the family over the years. The trip was lengthy, extending from the Rocky Mountains in Idaho to the Gulf of California. Angus finally wrote it down sometime in the late 1870s. It was published later, entitled, "An Indian Girl's Story of a Trading Expedition to the Southwest About 1841," edited by Winona Adams. The story incorporates many incidents and episodes, or small vignettes. Some of the episodes are about bloody struggles and pitched battles, but there are also informative and pictorial sketches of flora and fauna; grasses, berries, coyotes, horses, birds, geography, ethnography, adventure, a bit of veterinary, and Catherine's compassion. When she reached the Gulf of California she said:

> "we looked at the sea. There it was, that big mysterious thing. That deep of which I heard so much. We were at its side, but where were its back, head, and lungs, as they said it rose and breathed twice a day like man. All the water fowl that ever I saw were there, and the numbers more thick as they could swim. I thought the earth had not so many different bills. The sea was covered with them as a thick shower of summer hailstone covers our mountain prairies. They were no doubt gathered there for the winter and about to leave like ourselves for their distant home...."

Indian girls were well prepared for what was expected of them as women when they reached puberty. One of Catherine's sketches illustrates this: "Upon arriving at the third river, which was about three hundred paces broad, calm and of a gentle flow, all of us (women) bound our baggage in our leather lodges, put the children on the top and swam our best horses ashore holding cords in our teeth whose ends were tied to the lodges. The buffalo scalp bridle makes a soft wiry and light cord and is always preferred in this work to any other cords." (If there were more than one small child, the mother took them across, one by one, tied to the horse's back, making several trips until all were safely arrived. Catherine was responsible for her young brother's river crossing; her stepmother took her sister.)

Years later, when camping on the Pend d'Oreille River, Catherine heard screams from her children. Rushing to the riverbank she saw one of them sweeping down the "deep and flowing" river. She sprang into the water from the clay cliff, still in her clothing, and after a struggle caught her small daughter, whose little "tartan frock (was) making a safety collar around her neck." Unable to swim against the current with only one arm, Catherine "laid hold of the back of the head of the child in her teeth and thus the use of both hands was had, and required, to bring her after a long…and fatiguing swim ashore… (and, after) pressing and rolling the water out of her," Catherine's toddler, Christina, was soon mobile again. Christina was one of Catherine's older children. She recalled, much later, a trip taken, in 1852, from Flathead Valley to Colville (now in Washington). She said: "I was so small I had to be tied onto the saddle of the horse I rode." Children were introduced to horses early, consequently they became part of their lives, and they were comfortable with the large, big-toothed, strong, solid-hoofed animal.

A visitor to Fort Colville, Charles Wilson, an Englishman and surveyor, described the McDonald family as they were leaving on a hunting expedition: Catherine was "leading, perched high up on the curious saddle used by the women here, one of her younger daughters astride behind her and a baby swinging in its cradle from the pommel. Next came Miss

Christina, who is about seventeen, with her gaily beaded leggings and moccasins, gaudy shawl flying in the wind. She had a younger sister perched behind her and, in front a small brother… Next came the boys, two and two on horseback, and last McDonald himself, on his buffalo runner, surrounded by Indians," packhorses, and spare animals.

The "curious" saddle, on which Catherine was perched, was probably an adaptation of the high-bowed, Spanish war-saddle. The high horn saddle often held an awl case or horn- drinking cup, or other useful items that were thong tied onto, or strung from, the saddle horn. Catherine's horn held the baby's cradleboard, furnishing it with a natural rocking motion while they were en route. In this way, babies became aware of, and were familiarized with horses from infancy. The Nez Perce cradleboard had a high headboard that supplied protection, and was also a weather cover for the child.

Christina's beaded leggings were traditional, and could have been decorated with beaded designs of flowers, birds, triangles, butterflies, zigzags, diamonds, or animals. Leggings were worn for protection in travel. Her "gaudy shawl" might really have been a traditional Nez Perce dress with cape like sleeves that covered the elbows, and were fringed at the ends, appearing shawl like. The wing dress was usually worn with leggings. The Hudson's Bay Company began selling wing dresses with beaded or trade-cloth tops, made of wool felt or velveteen fabric.

The Spanish women, whom Catherine met on the expedition taken with her father, tried to induce her to come with them to California. Apparently some of the girls were to be married when they reached their destination. She wrote about them: "Being young, their women frequently untied my hair, which was long and fine and stroking it down invited me to go to California and be happy with them, but my native mountains and father were too dear to me to heed their plausible addresses." Catherine obviously cared about her father, and was close to him. He had chosen her name, and she probably learned to speak French from him. He taught her

Indian songs of the eastern United States, war songs, songs of chiefs, and dances. His French, and hers, would more than likely have been a patois. (A dialect, or speech that differs from the original.) Catherine spoke only French to her children. One of her sons, Duncan, said: "I speak French, not fluently, but good enough to talk to a Frenchman."

Distinguishing features and qualities of Catherine were revealed in the vignettes of her expedition story. She was observant, compassionate, resourceful, and determined in situations encountered along the trail during her journey. (Her journey began, "when the antelope were fawning in the last month of spring and the first month of summer," and ended, "in the fifth month of the year, which is the Kamas moon.") At one point in the journey, Catherine wanted to understand the machinations of a gray-headed man she observed. He, however, was not forthcoming with her. She continued to prod for an answer, and finally said: "I looked him full in his eyes intent to know why…Well my girl said he, as you are intent and pleasant, I will tell you."

Her will and determination carried into her marriage. A relative said, "When Catherine needed to, she would pack up the kids and they would go for awhile."

Angus noted, "Catherine has an excellent ear for the music of the white man as well as that of her red forefathers." He indulged the family with an expensive organ, but there is no mention of Catherine playing it. Maggie, one of their daughters, learned to play and sing to its accompaniment.

Catherine and Angus were married forty-seven years. They had twelve children and have many descendants. When she died in 1902, she was buried next to her husband in Mission Valley on the Flathead Reservation.

Catherine McDonald's tombstone showing the variant spelling of "MacDonald."

Chapter Five

THE McDONALD CHILDREN

John	born near Fort Hall, Idaho	1843
Christina	Payette River, Idaho	1847
Duncan	Flathead, Montana	March 30, 1849
Donald	Flathead, at Post Creek	February, 1851
Anne	Fort Colville, Washington	August16, 1853
Margaret	Fort Colville, Washington	December 1, 1855
Thomas	Fort Dearborn*	December 18, 1858
Alexander	Fort Colville, Washington	August 16, 1861
Archie	Fort Colville, Washington	July 19, 1863-1888
Joseph	Fort Colville, Washington	April, 1866
Angus C.	Fort Colville, Washington	April 11, 1868
Mary	Flathead Post	April 15, 1871
Angus P.	Fort Colville, Washington	1860-June 1924

Thomas was born at Fort Dearborn, past Helena, on the bend of the Missouri River during a buffalo hunt. He was washed in the river after delivery.

John McDonald. Courtesy K. Ross Toole Archives, University of Montana.

Duncan McDonald. Courtesy K. Ross Toole Archives, University of Montana.

Donald McDonald. Courtesy Fort Connah Restoration Society.

Anne "Annie" McDonald. Courtesy K. Ross Toole Archives, University of Montana.

Margaret "Maggie" McDonald. Courtesy K. Ross Toole Archives, University of Montana.

Thomas "Tom" McDonald. Courtesy K. Ross Toole Archives, University of Montana.

Archibald McDonald. Courtesy K. Ross Toole Archives, University of Montana.

Joseph McDonald. Courtesy K. Ross Toole Archives, University of Montana.

Angus C. McDonald and unidentified friend. Courtesy Fort Connah Restoration Society.

Mary McDonald. Courtesy K. Ross Toole Archives, University of Montana.

Angus P. McDonald. Courtesy K. Ross Toole Archives, University of Montana.

The McDonald Family Cemetery is located close to Post Creek about a half-mile east of the site of the Fort Connah trading post.

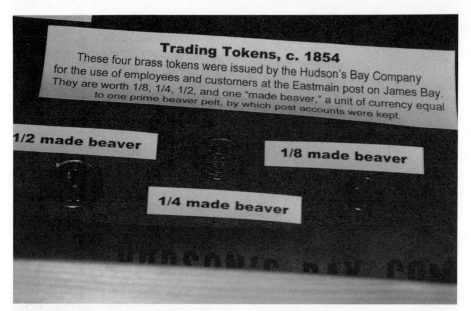

Trading Tokens, c. 1854

These four brass tokens were issued by the Hudson's Bay Company for the use of employees and customers at the Eastmain post on James Bay. They are worth 1/8, 1/4, 1/2, and one "made beaver," a unit of currency equal to one prime beaver pelt, by which post accounts were kept.

1/2 made beaver

1/8 made beaver

1/4 made beaver

Several knives, a sharpening stone, a set of spurs, a hide stamp and coins actually used at Fort Connah, part of the collection of George Knapp of Missoula, are in a display depicting Fort Connah's history at the Ninepipes Museum of Early Montana.

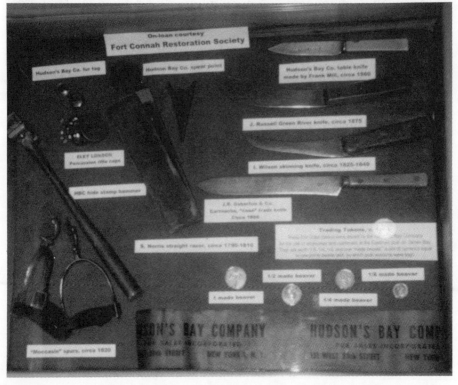

Book Three

ADDITIONAL ASPECTS OF THE FORT CONNAH STORY

Chapter Six

THE FUR TRAPPER

The fur trader and the trapper are unique in their position and contribution to American history. Not only were they explorers, frontiersman, and participants in a unparalleled adventures, but they also established trade and commerce routes and preceded the missionary, the gold-seeker, the cattleman and the settler in this country's history. Called by Hiram Chittendon "the true pathfinder of the west," he played his part and quickly vanished from the scene. "The feet of a nation walked his half-obliterated trails,

> The course of empire followed his solitary pathways
> to the western sea. In a few years, he set his imprints
> forever on the map of the United States, affected the
> destiny of nation,
> changed the future of the continent, bequeathed a tradition
> of heroic exploration." (Cleland, p. 5 and 12)

The description of the trapper's appearance is given by Hiram Chittenden:

> –dark skin, rough and hardy physique
> hair: long, coarse, bushy, shoulder length
> low-crowned woolen hat, and fringed buckskin pants
> footwear: deer or elk skin
> leather belt held butcher knife and pistols
> bullet pouch around neck

powder horn from shoulder, bullet mold, ball screw, wiper and awl.
gun stick and rifle

sometimes a deer overshirt–chin to thighs (soaked in water, wrung out, dried became a veritable coat of mail resisting Indian arrows.)
(Chittenden, p. 20)

Trapping beaver: a strong steel trap, weighing about five pounds and costing twelve to sixteen dollars and with a swivel chain attached was planted in about three to four inches of water. The chain was fastened to a strong stick which was then driven into the stream bed. Over the trap a twig was set above the surface of the water and baited with castor, a derivative of the sexual organs of the beaver. The beaver reaches for the bait, it springs the trap, dives into deep water, struggles and drowns.

Beaver skinning is an art. The skin is slit, removed and dried on a willow hoop, scraped, and smoked for 10-12 hours. Skins are then folded with fur inside, packed in bundles, tied with green thongs, which contract and when dry become almost as strong as iron bands. (Cleland, p. 12-14)

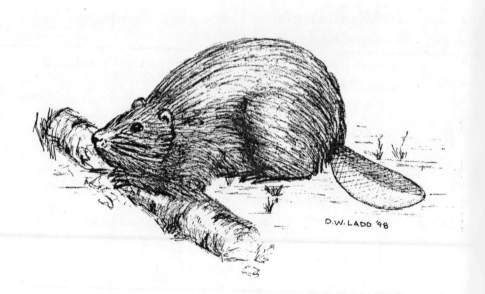

D.W. LADD '98

THE OREGON TREATY

The Oregon Territory, which extended from northern California to Alaska, was disputed by Great Britain, the United States, Russia and Spain. However, Russia and Spain withdrew their claims: Russia in 1824, Spain in 1819. In 1818 Great Britain and the United States agreed to joint occupancy. Missionaries were helping settle the area, and in 1842 the first emigrant train arrived over the Oregon Trail. With settlers pouring into the area, the United States inching toward war with Mexico and Great Britain dealing with famine in Ireland and war in India, a settling of the disputed area became imperative to both countries. The Oregon Treaty, signed in 1846, defined the boundary between Canada and the United States as the 49th parallel, an extension of the Canadian-American boundary that had been fixed in 1818 only as far as the Rockies. The Hudson's Bay Company was not satisfied with this arrangement, feeling that the boundary settlement sacrificed a trade with an annual profit of over 40,000 pounds from Fort Vancouver and other posts in the surrendered area, including Fort Connah.

The Puget Sound Agriculture Company was formed in 1838-39 to separate the Hudson's Bay Company's agricultural from more legitimate commerce. "The connexion between the two companies consisted in the Hudson's Bay Company being the large purchaser of the agricultural produce of the Puget Sound Company and the Governor and Dep. Governor of Hudson's Bay Company and governor in chief of their Territories became the Agents of the Puget Sound Company the business of which is carried on under a "Deed of Settlement." (Sir George Simpson, 3 December 1852.)

Sir George maintained that the rights of the Hudson's Bay Company and the Puget Sound Company had never been defined, but those companies believed that they were entitled to far more in remunerations than the United States was willing to admit. However, in order to avoid strife which would be injurious to the peace and good order of the territory, "the Companies are willing to cede their rights and possessions to the U.S.

Government for the sum of One Million dollars – less than half of the value as by the annexed estimate." (Sir George Simpson)

Twenty-five years passed before the final settlement of the Oregon Treaty. By then the value of the properties had markedly declined. In September 1869, a joint commission awarded the Company $450,000 for its rights and $200,000 for the Puget Sound Agricultural Company's holdings. This ended the long history of the Hudson's Bay Company in Oregon and Washington Territory including northwest Montana.

FINAN MCDONALD

"A frightening, red-haired, red-bearded giant of a Scotsman", Big Finan McDonald, distant cousin to Angus McDonald of Mission Valley, was an especially colorful member of an always colorful profession, and one of the first trappers and traders to enter what is now western Montana. His presence in the Flathead country several decades before Angus arrived is memorable to the Flathead, or Salish Indians, with whom he traded and socialized. "Big Finan was six feet, four inches tall, with broad shoulders, bushy whiskers and red hair, which for some years, had not felt the scissors and which, sometimes fell over his face and shoulders, giving him a wild and uncouth appearance," (Cox, *Adventures on the Columbia river,* as quoted in Hunter, p. 92).

Finan was born in Scotland in 1782. "He belonged to a highly respectable family" one of his colleagues noted and when a young lad emigrated to Canada with his father. Angus of Mission Valley claimed kinship with him many years later when he referred to Finan as "bough of the same tree as my own." (McDonald, *Items of the* West, p. 194*)* Finan joined the North West Company and traveled to the Flathead country in the Columbia region. His legendary conflict with a buffalo bull, which he wrestled to the ground when it tried to gore him, made Finan a respected hero to both Indians and whites. His temper was fiery, and even a suspected slight infuriated him, and he would lapse into a "ludicrous melange of Gaelic, English, French and a half-dozen Indian dialects." (Cox, *Adventures* *on the Columbia* as quoted in Hunter, p. 92.) McDonald frequently, for the mere love of fighting, accompanied the Flatheads in their war excursions against the Blackfeet. His eminent bravery endeared him to the whole tribe. Consequently, the Blackfeet resented his fiery participation, and one Piegan chief boasted that he would "get the red hair's scalp."

Finan, the trusted lieutenant of North West's Fur Company's David Thompson, traveled up the Kootenai River near present-day Libby, Montana, and in 1807 established the first fur-trading post in Flathead territory, Kootenai Post. He also accompanied Thompson when that noted geographer was mapping the Columbia River in 1810-1811. Finan married Margaret, daughter of Pend'd Oreille chief, *Chin-chay-nay-whey.* Their daughter, Helen was the wife of Richard Grant, bourgeois at Fort Hall when young Angus McDonald was stationed there in the early 1840's. From her Angus learned of the exploits of Finan and of Helen's childhood among the Flatheads. This relationship surely facilitated Angus' introduction to and presence among the Flatheads when he arrived in their valley in 1847.

In 1826 Finan retired and moved his family to Canada. On the way he was horribly wounded by a buffalo bull, but the indomitable old "Red Hair" survived to become a partner in the company. The family settled on a farm in Glencarry County where Finan became prominent in regional affairs.

DAVID THOMPSON

David Thompson (1770-1957), considered the greatest nineteenth century surveyor in North America, Western Canada, and Northwest United States, apprenticed himself to the Hudson's Bay Company at age fourteen. Twelve years later, he blazed a new route to Lake Athabasca for the Company. However, in 1797, dissatisfied with Hudson's Bay, Thompson left that organization and joined the rival North West Company, and in 1804 he became a partner. He surveyed the Mississippi headwaters for his employers, crossed the Canadian Rockies in 1807 to the source of the Columbia River. He was criticized, however, for not arriving there before the Lewis and Clark Expedition and John Jacob Astor's Astorians. "David

Thompson has been maligned for this period in his life although he did what a careful, prudent man would do in similar circumstances and he did it in a workmanlike manner. His achievements have been misunderstood by persons unfamiliar with his problems, which were a combination of geography and economics." (Smiley, *The Dalliance of David Thompson,* p. 47.)

Thompson was exploring the areas that are now Washington, Idaho and Montana in 1808-1810. He trapped and traded along the Kootenai River in Northwest Montana near present-day Libby, Troy and Lake Koocanusa, and reported in his journal that game and fish were so scarce that they nearly starved to death. Kullyspeel House, on the east shore of Lake Pend' d Oreille was built by Thompson in 1809, and the following year he established Salish (or Seelish) House) near present-day Thompson Falls, which is named for him.

This amazing man was the first white man to travel the full length of the Columbia River, the first white man to view and record Flathead Lake and the first to climb present-day Mount Jumbo and map the Missoula Valley, 1811. In 1812, Thompson, known to his Indian friends as *Koo-Koo-Sint,* the Star Gazer, visited the Flathead camp at the mouth of the Jocko River. When he retired that year he devoted his time to preparing a map which became the basis for all subsequent maps of western Canada. From 1816 to 1826 Thompson surveyed the U.S.-Canadian boundary between the St. Lawrence River and Lake of the Woods. He retired from the North West Company and died in poverty in 1857 in Montreal. His works were not published until 1916. (Graves, p. 13-15)

JACQUES (JOCKO) FINLAY

Jocko Finlay, an employee of the North West Company who traveled and traded with David Thompson, was born in 1768 in Montreal, the son of James Finlay, Sr., who married a Chippewa Indian woman. Jocko's French father was one of the founders of the North West Fur Company. In 1798, Jocko was at the North West post at Bow River in Canada when 150 hostile Indians attacked. Jocko, with three other men, distinguished themselves by holding off the Indians until help arrived. Jocko traded successfully with the Flathead Indians in those early 1800's, and in 1809 he and David Thompson built Kullyspel House on Pend d'Oreille Lake. Jocko was in charge of Spokane House, an Hudson's Bay post until his death in 1818. His name is perpetuated in the Mission Valley by Jocko Valley, Jocko River, Jocko Agency and by Finley Point named for Jocko's grandson, Piol Finley. (Note: change of spelling of "Finlay".)

THE NATIONAL BISON RANGE

The National Bison Range, a protected reserve southeast of St. Ignatius, is home to over 500 bison as well as deer, bighorn sheep, antelope and elk. Sixty-million bison had once covered the Great Plains, but white settlers and commercial hunters had almost exterminated the great herds by 1880. On the Flathead Reservation, however, a small herd remained. How did it get there?

Several stories offer explanation. One popular version: "Sam WalkingCoyote, a young Pend d'Oreille, living among the Salish, was hunting with the Blackfeet in the Milk River country about early 1870's. While there he married a Blackfeet, but because he already had a wife back home on the Flathead Reservation, he was living in defiance of tribal rules against polygamy. Some of his Blackfeet friends suggested that he take several bison across the mountains to the Flathead country as a peace offering. He trained six of the animals to follow his horse and trailed them into the Mission Valley. As Walking Coyote continued living among the Salish his bison multiplied. In 1884 he decided to sell his heard to Michel Pablo and Charles Allard. Walking Coyote took his $3,000 in cash to Missoula. After several days of wild celebration he was found murdered beneath the Higgins St. bridge, his money gone.

In the Flathead tribal tradition, it was a man named Latati who brought the bison onto the reservation. When young Latati's father died, his mother married Walking Coyote, who sold the bison to the two ranchers unbeknownst to his new family.

By the time Charles Allard died in 1896, the Pablo-Allard herd had grown to more than 300 animals. Pablo held on to his share of the herd, but Allard's heirs sold theirs. In 1907, as the government prepared to open the reservation to white homesteaders, Pablo sold his 600 bison to Canadian buyers, but first the herd had to be rounded up. About the time of the roundup, which took five years to get it into Canada, William T. Hornaday and members of the American Bison Society began planning a preserve for the animals somewhere on the Flathead Reservation. President Theodore Roosevelt signed the enabling bill, and the society raised the needed funds to purchase the nucleus herd of forty bison. Most of these came from Kalispell's Conrad family, who had bought them from Allard a decade earlier. The refuge at Moiese was the first area in Montana established specifically to preserve a single species." – Don Spritzer, *Roadside History of Montana,* (p. 169-171)

THE MISSIONS

In the 1820's some Iroquois Indians who had been "Christianized" by the "blackrobes", came to live among the Flatheads residing in the Bitterroot Valley. These Iroquois were skilled trappers who had followed the fur trade west and had been converted by the Jesuit missionaries. They introduced the gentle Flathead to Catholic prayer and ritual, and told them stories about Christ. The Flatheads were so impressed with this new "medicine" that, they along with several Nez Perce, sent four delegations through hazardous country to St. Louis to plea for the Blackrobes to come to them. Father Pierre Jean de Smet, S.J., a young Jesuit missionary from Belgium, answered the call, and in 1841 he established St. Mary's Mission on the Bitterroot River near present-day Stevensville. K. Ross Toole observed that "DeSmet himself admitted that behind the Flatheads' intense desire for blackrobes lay a conviction that through such offices they could defeat their enemies and preserve themselves... especially against the dreaded and hated Blackfeet" (Toole, pp. 60-61). For about five years the little mission flourished as the priests attempted to introduce their Indian friends to farming and to an intensive religious instruction.

However, when the Indians returned from their buffalo hunt in the summer of 1846, their attitude changed to savagery toward the missionaries for several reasons. For five years the Flatheads had enjoyed good hunting and good fortune in repelling their enemies, but Father de Smet, in his zeal to convert, had mentioned that he intended to found a mission to the Blackfeet, the hated enemy. By 1850, relations were strained, encouraged by rumors and suspicions planted by some fur traders and trappers including Angus McDonald. Unfortunately, the head of the mission became involved in tribal politics and in 1850 the rift was seen as unbridgeable. The priests closed the mission, leased it to trader Major John Owen, departed not to return until 1866. (Toole, pp. 60-62.)

In the Mission Valley St. Ignatius was established by Jesuit Fathers de Smet and Adrian Hoecken. The first mission was initially sited on the present Idaho-Washington border in 1845, but when this location proved unsuitable due to heavy snow and flooding, it was moved in 1854 to its present site, a place known as *"Snieleman"* (a Salish word meaning rendezvous) about six miles south of Fort Connah. In 1864 four Sisters of Providence of Montreal opened a girls' boarding school and a "hospital" in the convent-school. The present church of St. Ignatius, a National Historic Site was built in 1891.

CHRISTMAS AT POST CREEK

(From "Old Time Christmas Days as Spent on Post Creek")

Christmas in the years past on Post Creek was always to be looked forward to and a time to be remembered. For here is where the Hudson's Bay Company did its largest trading with the three grandest tribes in the Northwest – the Flatheads, Kootenais and Upper Pend d'Oreilles. Old Millie Revais, esteemed elder of the Pend d'Oreille, told of the gathering held on the first Christmas, a time when the whole week of Christmas was spent in merry-making. Here close to the purest stream on the whole reservation, the Indians came and, sitting around huge campfires, they would recount the adventures of the past few months since the commencement of the trapping and hunting season. And here they would bring their first seasons harvest to barter with the representatives of the Hudson's Bay Company.

The word would go out in late summer that the braves should prepare themselves for a big hunt, *lult chines-chilpini,* and at the end of a given number of moons, they were to return with the skins of what had been killed, and all were to gather with their spoils to the cabins which were then being built by some Pale Faces near to where the then trail crossed what is now known as Post Creek. In fact, sometimes as early as three weeks before the specified time, bands of Indians came riding in with their skins

A brave would lay his skins before the traders, they would be examined as to quality, and he was told that they were worth so much flour, or coffee, or sugar and salt. There was no wrangling as the Indian believed he was offered what his skins were thought to be honestly worth. These trades usually began one week before Christmas day and on Christmas eve all business was completed. The next day, Christmas, the families were treated to a feast. At first the Indians scarcely comprehended the reason why the White Man, in the dead of winter, should choose to select such a time to celebrate some event; but as each milestone was reached in the lives of these people, they began to look forward to Christmas, *kutunt-sgalgalt,* the Flathead for "holy day".

There were few white men in their midst then: Angus McDonald, a whole-souled, big hearted Scotchman, Louis Ashley, a French Canadian, and two brothers, Scots Jim and Patrick Finley. All four of these men intermarried into the tribes. The Captain of the Company told the purpose of the establishment of the post. "He told how the pale-faced brothers and sisters of these people who lived in the East, where it was very cold, wanted the skins of the animals roaming the forests of this wild country with which to keep warm; that the skins were made into garments and coverings; that they could not be had in the section where these pale-faced people lived because there were no animals like those in the wilds here roaming there;

and that he had to offer them in exchange for their skins a snowy, white substance, flour, which they made into "bread" . Also he had to offer them tea and coffee, the former looking like a dried weed, and the coffee like a very small black pebble. Both of these put into hot, boiling water, the latter first crushed with a rock, would give them a pleasant fluid to drink. To prove this was true he asked them to partake of the bread, tea and coffee with sugar and salt on their buffalo meat. They timidly partook of the offerings and awaited results." (Ranft, Christmas at Post Creek", p. 6-7)

Millie Revais said it was at least half an hour before anyone said anything. Shortly, Eneas, chief of all the Kootenais...arose and announced that they would all smoke the pipe of peace, and if at the end of the smoke they were not all dead, the trading would begin. Silently they smoked and when nothing occurred to make them sorry that they had tasted of the white man's food, nothing happened save the desire to have more of it and the first bartering between the Pend 'd Oreilles, Kootenais and Flatheads occurred. As each succeeding year was reached and passed these Indians became more intimately acquainted with Christmas, what it was, and what it meant to all mankind.

(From Ranft. William Q. "Old -Time Christmas Days as Spent on Post Creek" *Western Homeseeker,*vol, 1, no. 3pp. 6-7

Missoula, Montana, Western Homeseeker Publishing Co. 1905.

THE PEOPLE'S CENTER

The Peoples' Center, a place encompassing the melding of two cultures, is located on U.S. Highway 93 just north of Pablo, Montana. Here proud Indian traditions are honored within present-day society. This is where the people gather to share, to learn, to tell their stories not only to each other but also to visitors. Craftsmen and craftswomen continue to do beadwork and quill work on buckskin which has been scraped and prepared by hand. Families still speak their native languages and exhibits depict the ancient lore and legends of the tribes. While immersing themselves in their own culture, the people have adapted to the current society in which they live, have formed their own tribal government, developed a viable economy, established a tribal college – Salish Kootenai College – at Pablo, and maintain health and social services throughout the reservation.

For years this sign along U.S. Highway 93 just to the west of the Fort Connah site drew attention to area's history.

Book Four

IMAGES OF
FORT CONNAH'S PAST

Chapter Seven

ARTISTS AT FORT CONNAH

Two artists who came to trans-mountain western Montana and
into the Flathead region during the 1850s and 1860s were Peter Tofft and
Gustavus Sohon. They sketched and painted scenes of the area and its
people, leaving behind a pictorial history of the region during that period.

Peter Peterson Tofft (1825-1901) was born in Kolding, Denmark.
At age seventeen, after a solid classical education, he took off on his own,
setting to sea on a whaling ship. He eventually landed in California just in
time to catch "gold fever". He found modest success in mining and after a
trip back to Denmark, returned to California. During that time we hear the
first mention of Tofft sketching and painting. While holding an assortment
of jobs along the Pacific coast, he exhibited some of his work in San
Francisco. During that time, a friend introduced him to Albert Bierstadt as
"a fellow painter", but Tofft demurred: "No, no, not a painter but a daub."
Bierstadt was a German born, American artist, who painted grand western
landscapes and geological formations, and made them appear even more
magnificent because of his technical skills and artistic vision. He was elected
into the National Academy of Design in New York after a well-received
showing of his paintings and drawings, done while on General Fredrick
Lander's survey for a road from Fort Laramie (Wyoming) to the Pacific. He
was a popular and successful artist. Meeting Bierstadt was clearly
uncomfortable for Tofft. Throughout his career, he was always conscious of

his lack of training. Years later, he confessed to a friend: "I sketch (my friends say) with considerable power – but I commenced too late in life to acquire the knowledge necessary for a finished picture." Tofft's paintings, however, are valuable. They have proven to be reliably accurate and unequivocal in detail, although they may be somewhat technically deficient.

Tofft, again lured by gold, traveled to Montana in 1865. He saw the Cabinet Mountains, Thompson Falls, and Horse Prairie (present day Plains) as he followed the Clark River on his journey into Montana. While resting at the Flathead Reservation, he sketched and painted a number of scenes, including the St. Ignatius Mission, and the Hudson's Bay Trading post, Fort Connah. A present day art critic had this to say about Tofft's painting of Fort Connah: "The artist does capture the quiet majesty of the Mission range and the inviting warmth of the frontier community, where log cabins and skin lodges share the protection of the valley floor."

The end of the year found him in the Bitterroot Valley, in the company of Major John Owens, who operated the Fort Owen trading post. Owen's view of Tofft and his drawings was: "He has taken some very pretty sketches of different parts of the valley – He does Well for an Amateur – he Seems to have good taste and is Without doubt a Natural Artist – Success to him in his artistical pursuits." In February, Tofft left Fort Owen on snowshoes, headed for the mining district of Elk Lodge.

An unfortunate fall from his horse forced an end to his prospecting pursuit. Painting became his only vocation. He visited mining settlements, but this time drew and painted them. He spent time in the capital of the territory, Virginia City, and Bannack, which had been the first capital of the territory. Tofft sold sixteen of his paintings to Granville Stewart, who was active in mining and later in ranching, and, while there, the painter attracted several other patrons. He sold his work for five dollars, in gold, per picture. He was well received in Helena where they wanted him to stay. Some said Tofft was deserving of lucrative patronage.

He made arrangements with Acting Governor Thomas Meagher,

who wanted to use some of Tofft's paintings and drawings to illustrate a travel article he intended to write. The article was to appear in "Harper's New Monthly Magazine" entitled, "Rides Through Montana." It was published in October 1867, and was probably one of the first illustrated stories about Montana featured in a national publication. Later, in 1870, the "Illustrated London News" used an engraving based on Tofft's painting, "Three Forks of the Missouri River." His watercolor called, " Unionville," (a mining camp near Helena) was again the basis of a lithograph. It appeared in "Pencil Sketches of Montana," by Alfred Mathews.

Tofft left the United States in 1868 and never returned to Montana. He lived and visited in the Middle East, New York, California and the east coast of the United States. He died in London in 1901. The collection of historical drawings, which feature Montana's land marks, are Peter Tofft's rich legacy. His work furnished a visual record of the old Northwest.

Gustavus Sohon came to America from Tilset, Germany. He joined the U.S. Army ten years later, serving under Captain George B. McClellan. The company was stationed in the Bitterroot Valley, where Sohon, was a member of the survey crew, commanded by Lieutenant John Mullan. His assignment was: artist, barometer-carrier and observer. The team's job was to find a navigable rail route through the northern Rockies. They set up their camp about ten miles from Fort Owen in the valley, where they built four log houses for their winter quarters. The little neighborhood was called, "Cantonment Stevens." In 1853 it was the subject of one of Sohon's unique sketches, and it was later made into a lithograph.

Sohon learned to speak Salish quickly, and was reassigned as one of the interpreters for Governor Isaac Stevens when he settled the treaties with the Northwestern tribes. Sohon made watercolor and pencil drawings of the Indians during those meetings. He sketched the mounted Nez Perce parade as they entered the council ground, and also made drawings during the council of the Flathead Indians, where their first treaty with the United States was negotiated. His sketch makes clear why the Indians call the council site: "Where the trees have no lower limbs."

The artist also prepared field sketches, maps, meteorological data, and landscape sketches with noted landmarks. One of his sketches shows the survey party headed for Fort Dalles. It is called, "The Pack-Train Crossing the Snow Covered Bitterroot Mountains." In 1854, Sohon drew pencil portraits of Flathead chief, Alexander (a Pend d'Orielle); Adolphe (a Flathead leader); Lame Bull (a Piegan Chief); and two Iroquois guides, Aeneas and Pierre, who were helpful in bringing Christian missions to the Northwest tribes. Aeneas led Father de Smet across the Rockies to the Flatheads. Pierre hurried ahead to alert the Indians of the priest's arrival. John Ewers, a western historian, said Sohon had a "great talent for portraiture that justifies ranking him among the most able artist who interpreted the plains and Rockies during the Nineteenth Century."

Nothing is known about his education or art training. Before his army enlistment he had been a photographer, woodcarver, and bookbinder. There is no record of art productions made by him after leaving the army. During his time of duty in the west, Sohon provided an accurate geographical record of northwestern areas, and augmented the pictorial history of its people and events.

A KEY ARTIST OF THE ERA

Alfred Jacob Miller (1810-1874) drew and painted a series of scenes from the fur trade that have given us incredible insights into the way of life during the era of the fur trade and although no record exists to indicate that he visited Fort Connah, his paintings assist our understanding of those times. Miller was an eye-witness to the trade during the short corridor of time when the American fur trade flourished. He painted what he saw from on-location experience. He sketched mountain men, Indians, the fur trade rendezvous, socialization at the rendezvous, wagon caravans carrying furs and supplies for trade and barter, portraits of attendees, and landmark formations along the way to the rendezvous, such as Chimney Rock and the

Tetons, etc. (A rendezvous was a yearly gathering of traders, mountain men and trappers. They met to buy and sell furs and supplies, and to socialize.)

A wealthy Scottish nobleman, William Drummond Steward, hired Miller to accompany him, and paint, on a trip west. The trip planned was to the Green River region of what is now Wyoming. Steward wanted him to produce a collection of paintings from the trip. Photography was not available until the 1850s, and artists, like Miller, filled the gap. Miller was an American artist from Baltimore, Maryland. He had trained in Rome and Paris, and with Thomas Sulley before going overseas. He was deemed a Romantic painter because of his use of color (pale, misty, mountains against brownish foregrounds) and exotic or unusual subject matter. Stewart looked his work over, and then hired him.

Stewart and Miller joined forces with a large caravan of trappers, traders and Indians in 1837, and headed for their trip to the Rocky Mountains. Miller's sketches from the journey were turned into finished oil paintings, and eighty-three drawings and watercolors. They are valuable works of art, which contribute to the knowledge of the West. He allows us to glimpse the lives of traders and trappers, providing opportunity to see and examine what we have heard and read. Miller's pictures are an important segment of the visual history of the fur trade.

Editor's Note – *Several photographs collected by the Fort Connah Restoration Society linking the persons and activities of succeeding generations of Angus McDonald to the Fort Connah story provide insight into the family's rich Scottish-Native American heritage. We are indebted to both the Society and to the K. Ross Toole Archives at the University of Montana for these photographs.*

Joseph McDonald, son of Angus McDonald, and family in an undated photograph. Courtesy Fort Connah Restoration Society.

The packstring was fundamental to the transport of supplies. Here, in another undated photograph, Charles McDonald, son of Joseph McDonald and grandson of fur trader Angus McDonald is shown leading a string in the mountains. Courtesy Fort Connah Restoration Society.

Another undated yet intriguing photograph of Angus McDonald's descendants depicts this camp scene. In the photograph are Old Bonapart, Florence McDonald in costume, Mary McDonald Swaney, Edward, Charlie, Dan and Bennie, plus Father Joe. Courtesy K. Ross Toole Archives, University of Montana.

Angus P. McDonald and Maggie McDonald, children of fur trader Angus McDonald. Courtesy Fort Connah Restoration Society.

Joseph McDonald, son of Angus McDonald. Courtesy Fort Connah Restoration Society.

From left are Susan Magpie, John McDonald, grandson of Angus McDonald,
Florence McDonald Smith, granddaughter of Angus McDonald, and Mary C.
McDonald Swaney. The grandchildren's father was Joseph McDonald. Courtesy
Fort Connah Restoration Society.

Tom McDonald, son of fur trader Angus McDonald and his wife, Christine, standing, an shown with an unidentified friend. Courtesy Fort Connah Restoration Society.

Duncan McDonald, son of fur trader Angus McDonald in an undated photograph taken in the Mission Valley. Courtesy Fort Connah Restoration Society.

Duncan McDonald, son of fur trader Angus McDonald. Courtesy Fort Connah Restoration Society.

Duncan McDonald, son of fur trader Angus McDonald. Courtesy Fort Connah Restoration Society.

Artifacts and memorabilia from Fort Connah itself, including many personal items of Angus McDonald, are on display at the Ninepipes Museum of Early Montana.

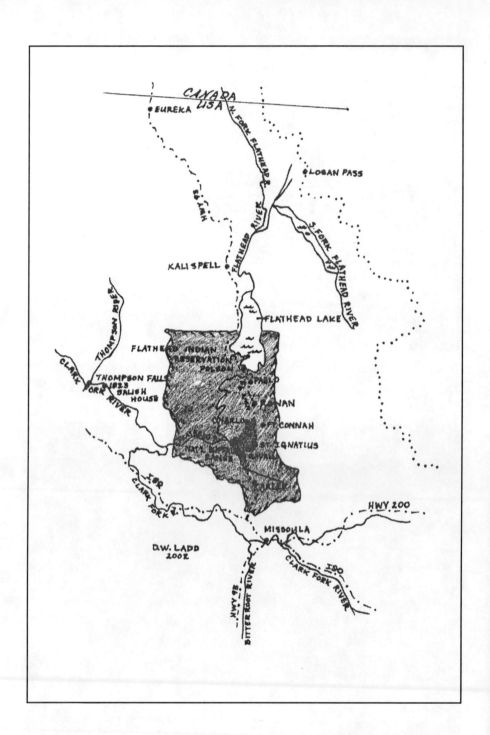

Book Five

FORT CONNAH: ITS FUTURE

Only the major store building at Fort Connah remains standing and it likely is the oldest standing man-made structure in the state of Montana. This photograph taken in the late 1960s shows the building in a state of disrepair that sparked efforts to get a restoration effort going.

RESTORING FORT CONNAH

The run-down old cabin, standing lonely and forgotten in the shadow of the Mission Mountains in view of U.S. Highway 93, was a silent and shadowy sentinel of a long past era in Montana history. A highway road sign indicates that this was the site of Fort Connah, the last Hudson's Bay fur trading post in Montana. Many of the residents on the Flathead Reservation are direct descendants of the colorful Highlander, Angus McDonald, a fur trader for the Hudson"s Bay's Company, who built the post in 1847 and retired nearby when it closed in 1871. Because Fort Connah has both Native American and European historic and cultural values, the old post is a National Historic Register Site. Concern that the historic old building might disappear into oblivion led interested persons to form the Fort Connah Restoration Society in 1975.

Soon the old post awakened from its slumber as enthusiastic volunteers removed log by log and replaced each one to give the little cabin a fresh and durable reconstruction complete with a new shake roof. Besides being one of the original buildings, this log structure is of special interest because it is constructed of "Red River frame" or "posts on the sill" construction. This consist of upright logs at the corners, doors and windows with horizontal squared logs filling the spaces in between. This style of log architecture was common to many Hudson's Bay posts. Walter McDonald, a direct descendant of Angus and his Nez Perce wife, Catherine, inherited the land on which the cabin rests. Walter sold the land except for four acres around the cabin, which he reserved and donated to the restoration project. Memberships in the Society, supplemented by several grants, financed the project. The Society has now purchased eighteen acres and is continuing its efforts to restore and refurbish the building to the period of the mid-1850's and to maintain the McDonald Family Cemetery.

Plans call for the original buildings to be rebuilt according to their 1850 appearance and will be furnished in the style of the Hudson's Bay 's Company and the Rocky Mountain fur trade. To carry out the restoration with concern for authenticity, the findings of historians, archeologists and architects will be analyzed, and combined with ecological and cultural considerations to then determine the course of development the site will

Members of the Fort Connah Restoration Society's first board of directors were (from left) Preston Miller, Dorothy Roske, Cornelia Francis, Walter McDonald, Rod Wamsley and Ray Harbin. This photo was taken in 1975.

take. Plans also provide for the erection of a modern Interpretive Center and public parking.

To help restore old Fort Connah, contributions can be sent to:

Ft. Connah Restoration Society

P.O. Box 56

Charlo, Montana 59824

Family memberships are $25.00 and General Memberships are $10.00 (tax deductible).

Editor's Note – While restoration efforts at the Fort Connah site have begun, much work remains to be accomplished. In this sequence of photographs we show some of the preliminary tasks the Fort Connah Restoration Society, utilizing volunteer assistance, undertook to stabilize the one major building remaining at the site.

The building upon completion of the initial restoration work.

APPENDIX

HISTORIC TIME LINE
FOR FORT CONNAH

1600's: Ancestors of today's Montana Indians arrived. Kootenai may have been first of the present-day tribes.

1670: Hudson's Bay Company given royal charter and monopoly on the fur-trade.

1700's: Principal Tribes are: Kalispel, Flathead, Pend O'Reille, Shoshone, Gros Ventres, Nez Perce, Kootenai

1710: "Point Blankets" introduced by HBC.

1793: North West Company established by enterprizing Scots, headquarters at Montreal.

1800: NW Co. has 4,000 traders and trappers (Nor Westers) in field.

1805-06: Lewis & Clark Expedition lays Montana open to fur trade.

1808: David Thompson (No. West agent) traps and trades along Kootenai River in Northwest Montana.

1808: Finan McDonald (subordinate to Thompson) established Kootenai Post, Libby, Montana, for NW Co.

1809: Thompson builds Kullyspell House on Lake Pend d' Oreille. Travels up Clark Fork.

18 09: Thompson builds Salish House near Thompson Falls.

1809: Jacques (Jocko) Finaly is major trader for Thompson in this area .

Spokane House, established by Thompson.

1810-11: Joseph Howse establishes Ft. Howse at Flathead Lake, Hudson's Bay Company

1812: David Thompson visits Flathead camp on Jocko River.

1816: Angus McDonald born in Craig, Scotland.

1816: Thompson climbed Mt. Jumbo and mapped Missoula Valley.

1811-1824: active presence of HBC in Montana.

1821: HBC merger with North West Company ordered by British Government after violent competition.

1823: Flathead Post (second Saleesh House) established by Alexander Ross

1824-1830: Peter Skene Ogden, Head of Snake River Trade

1824: HBC built Columbia Department headquarters at Ft. Vancouver, Washington.

1825: Fort Colville established and named for HBC official, Andrew Colville.

1831-34: John Work, HBC, Snake River Brigade set out to trade with Salish and Blackfeet Indians.

1837: HBC pelts, received 26,735 – beaver declining – heavy trapping pressure.

— Fort. Hall, acquired by HBC.

1838: Angus McDonald emmigrates to Canada from Scotland

1839: Angus McDonald – Employed by HBC, assigned to Flathead Country as apprentice clerk.

1841: St. Mary's Mission opened in Bitterroot Valley by Jesuit priests.

1842: Angus and Catherine married at Fort Hall in civil ceremony performed by Bourgeois Richard Grant.

1846-47: Flathead Post moved east to new post, started construction by Neil McLean McArthur – in service to the HBC as apprentice clerk at old Flathead Post on the Flathead River.

1846: 49th Parallel: Oregon Treaty with U.S. and Canada extends boundary to Puget Sound.

1846: U.S. receives Oregon wilderness.

1847: Angus McDonald succeeds Neil McArthur as clerk at the Flathead Post, renames the post Fort Connah.

1848: Territory of Oregon organized.

1849: Duncan McDonald born at Fort Connah.

1850: Official declaration by Supt. Of Indian Affairs for Oregon Territory stated in effect that HBC posts were not to operate within Indian territory under penalty (Intercourse Act of 1834).

1850: Pack trains leave twice a year from Fort Connah to Fort Colville in Washington State.

1850's: Day of beaver fur trade closing in western Montana. Beaver hats out of fashion, but interest in leather for clothing and animal tack.

1850: Major John Owen receives St. Mary's Mission property. Fort Owen becomes trade competitor to Fort Connah.

1851: Donald McDonald, son of Angus and Catherine, born at Fort Connah.

1852: Angus McDonald promoted to Chief Factor at HBC post, Fort Colville, Washington.

1853: Washington Territory formed, includes Fort Connah.

1853-61: Michel Ogden, son of Peter Skene Ogden, clerk and postmaster at Fort Connah; wife is Angelina, half-sister to Catherine McDonald.

1853-54: Captain Isaac I. Stevens, geographic survey for railroad: maps note Fort Connah.

1854: St. Ignatius Mission founded

1854: Angus and Catherine's marriage solemnized by Jesuit missionary.

1855: Treaty of Council Grove or "Hellgate Treaty" establishes Flathead Indian Reservation, site of Fort Connah

1855: Governor Isaac Stevens, Governor of Washington Territory, orders Fort Connah closed.

1855: Guarantees Indians protection against any claims of HBC growing out of trading post.

1855 : Blackfeet Indian Treaty with Confederated Flathead Tribes.

1855-56: Martial Law declared in Washington as hostilities increase between settlers and Indians.

1856: Fort Hall abandoned. Trade goods and supplies sent to Fort Connah.

1856-62: Major John Owens, U.S. Indian Agent to Flathead Reservation, 1865.

1857: HBC subject to parliamentary investigation.

1858-62: Mullan Road constructed from Fort Benton, Montana, to Walla Walla, Washington.

1858-64: Gold discovery brings migrations into region.

1860: Town of Hellgate springs up, forerunner to City of Missoula, Montana.

1860-61: U.S.and British survey crews mark 49th parallel as U.S. Canadian boundary from Columbia River to summit of the Rockies.

1861-65: Lachlan McLaurin, replaces Michel Ogden as custodian and clerk at Fort Connah.

1863: Treaty of Washington: Settlement of HBC claims under Oregon Treaty of 1846.

1863: Idaho Territory organized, includes Fort Connah.

1864: Montana Territory organized, includes Fort Connah, in Missoula County.

1865: Napoleon Fitzstubbs takes over Fort Connah as postmaster.

1866: Indian Agent seeks removal of Fort Connah Postmaster Nathaniel Fitzstubbs. (Not enforced).

1866-67: James McKenzie replaced Fitzstubbs: 1866-67. McKenzie, husband of Cristina McDonald, Angus' daughter.

1866-1871: Duncan McDonald, son of Angus, last clerk and custodian of Fort Connah.

1869: Joint British-American commission settles claims of HBC property loss ($450,000).

1871: Fort Connah closed by Duncan McDonald.

1872: Angus McDonald constructs family home adjacent to old Fort Connah.

1877: Nez Perce: Battle of the Big Hole, Aug. 9, 1877.

1889: Death of Angus McDonald, February at Post Creek, Mission Valley. Statehood for Montana.

1902: Death of Catherine McDonald, at Mission Valley.

1975: Formation of Fort Connah Restoration Society.

BIBLIOGRAPHY

•Adams., Winona, (ed.) "An Indian Girl's Story About a Trading Mission to the Southwest about 1841", *The Frontier,* X:4, May 1930.
•Alt, David, Hyndman, Donald, *Roadside Geology of Montana,* Missoula, Mountain Press, 1986.
•Alwin, John A., *Western Montana; a Portrait of the Land and Its People,* Montana Geographic Series, No. 5, Helena, Montana Magazine, Inc., 1983.
•Antrie, Albert, "Father Pierre Jean DeSmet," *Montana Magazine of Western History,* XIII:2, Spring, 1963.
•Alexrod, Alan, *Art of The Golden West,* Abbeville Press, Publishers, New York. 1990.
•Bigart, Robert, and Woodcock, Clarence , "Peter Tofft: Painter in the Wilderness," *Montana Magazine of Western History,* XXV;1, Autumn, 1975.
•Bleeker, Sonia, *Horsemen of The Western Plateau: The Nez Perce,* William Morrow and Company, New York. 1957.
•Blevins, Winfred, *Give Your Heart to The Haws: A Tribute to The Mountain Men,* Nash Publishing, Los Angeles, 1973.
•Bradshaw, Glenda Clay, Montana's Historical Markers, from an original text by Robert H. Fletcher, updated by Jan Aline, Montana Historical Society Press, Helena, 1989, 1994, 1999.
•Brown, Jennifer, "Ultimate Respectability: Fur Trade Children in the 'Civilized World'", *The Beaver* Spring, 1978.
•Brown, Mark H. and Felton, W.R., *The Frontier Years: L.A. Huffman,* Brownhall House, New York, 1955.
•Bryan, William Jr., *Montana's Indians: Yesterday and Today,* VXI(II), published by Montana Magazine, Helena, Montana, 1985.
•Burlingame, Merrill G., Ph.D, *The Montana Frontier*, State Publishing Company, Helena, Montana, 1942.

•Cheney, Roberta Carkeek, *Names on the Face of Montana*, Missoula: Mountain Press, 1983.

•Chittenden, Hiram Martin, *The American Fur Trader of the Far West*, Vol. 1, Lincoln: University of Nebraska ,1986

•Cleland, Robert Glass, *This Reckless Breed of Men: The Trappers and Fur Traders of the Southwest,* New York, Knopf, 1950.

•Cole, Jean Murray, *Exile in Wilderness-Life of Chief Factor Archibald McDonald, 1790-1853",* Ontario, Burns and McEachern Ltd., 1979 reviewed by Smith, Shirlee Ann, *The Beaver,* Spring, 1980

•Cordier, Rick, "My Son, My Son: Angus McDonald and Fort Connah" *Dovetail Magazine*, Ronan, 1973.

•Cross, Carlene, *The Undying West: A Chronicle of Montana's Camas Prairie*, Fulcrum Publishing, Golden, Colorado. 1999.

•Decker Papers, at St. Ignatius, Montana, family papers in possession of Eileen Decker.

•DeVoto, Bernard, *The Course of Empire,* New York, Bonanza, 1952.

    __ *Across the Wide Missouri*, New York, Bonanza Books, 1957.

• Dougherty, Michael, and Dougherty, Heidi Pfeil, *The Ultimate Montana Atlas and Travel Encyclopedia,* Bozeman, Ultimate Press, 2001.

•Dryden, Cecil, *Up the Columbia for Furs,* Caldwell, Caxton Printers, 1949

•Duncan, Dayton, *People of the West,* The West Project (based on Public Television Series, The West), New York, Little Brown, 1996.

•Dunning, Steve and Carol Lee, *Frontiers of Yesterday, Today and Tomorrow in Prose and Poetry,* Scholastic Book Services, 1961.

•Evans, Lucylle, *St. Mary's in the Rocky Mountains,* Stevensville, MT., Montana Creative Consultants, 1976.

•Ewers, John C. *"Iroquois Indians in the Far West",* Montana Magazine of Western History, xiii:2, Spring, 1963.

•Fanselow, Julie, *Traveling The Oregon Trail,* Falcon Press, Helena, Montana, 1992.

•Farley, John, *The Flathead Indians*, University of Oklahoma Press, 1974.

•Flathead Cultural Committee, *A Brief History of the Flathead Tribes*, 1993.

•Fletcher, Bob, Christopherson Ed, Colvert, Ed, *Montana's Historical Markers,* Missoula, Earthquake Press, 1970.

•Fletcher, Robert H., *Free Grass to Fences*, University Publishers, Inc., New York, 1960.

•Fort Connah Restoration Society, *Fort Connah: A Hudson's Bay Trading Company 1846-1871.* Pamphlet.

•Hakola, John W., Editor, *Frontier Omnibus*, Montana State University Press, Missoula, Montana, 1962.

•Hudson's Bay Company Archives, Provincial Archives of Manitoba, Canada, (i.e. HBCA/OAMB.239/a/1,fo.2,171154).

•"Hudson's Bay Co." Groliers, Multimedia Encyclopedia, Microsoft, 1981-1995.

•Gilbert, Bill, *The Trailblazers,* by the Editors of Time-Life Books, Old West Series, New Yorkk, 1973.

•Graves, F. Lee, *Montana Fur Trade Era,* Helena, Montana Magazine and American and World Geographic Publishing, 1994.

•Harrison, Michael, "Chief Charlo's Battle with Bureaucracy", *Montana Magazine of Western History,* X:4', Autumn 1960.

•Hollenstein, F. Walter, *"Letters to Mrs. Lorena Normandeau",* Dovetail Magazine, Ronan, 1974.

•Hudson's Bay Company Archives, Provincial Archives, Manitoba, Canada (ie. HBCA/PAM B.239/a/1,fo2,1M154)

•"Hudson's Bay Company", *The New American Desk Encyclopedia,* New York, Penguin, 1994.

•Hunter, James, *Scottish Highlanders, Indian Peoples Thirty Generations of a Montana Family,* Helena, Historical Society Press, 1996.

   —Angus McDonald, *A Scottish Highlander Among Indian Peoples,* Montana: The Magazine of Western History, Montana Historical Society. Winter 1977.

•Hurwitz, Howard L. *An Encyclopedic Dictionary of American History,* New York, Washington Square Press, 1970.

•James, Caroline, *The Nez Perce Women in Transition, 1877-1990,* University of Idaho Press, Moscow, Idaho. 1996.

•Jacobsen, Judy, Merrill, Andrea, *Montana Almanac,* Helena, Falcon, 1997.

•Johnson, Olga Weydemeyer, *Flathead and Kootenai: The River, the Tribes and the Regions' Traders,* Glendale, Arthur H. Clark, 1969.

•McDonald, Angus, "A Few Items of the West", (edited by Howay, F.W., Lewis, W.S., Mayers, J.A.), *Washington Historical Quarterly,* VIII, 1917.

•McDonald, Lois Halliday *"Fur Trade Letters of Francis Ermatinger*, Glendale: Arthur H. Clark.. 1980

•McRae, W.C., Jewell, Judy, *Montana Handbook,* Chico, Moon Publications, 1992.

•Moodie, D.S., Kaye, Bernie, *Ac Ko Mok Ki Map, The Beaver.* papers of the Fort Connah Restoration Society.

•Miller, Don, and Cohen, Stan, *Military Training Posts of Montana*, Missoula, Pictorial Histories Publishing, 1978.

•The Missoulian, *Reclaiming Destiny,* Missoula, Montana, February 27, 2000.

   —*Make Your Reservations*, June 10, 2001

   —*Change For The Better,* July 28, 2001

   —*Trail,* July 26, 2001

   —*School of Re-Education,* July 28, 2001

   —*Indian Trust Reform Mired,* September 19, 2001

   —*Out West: More Precious Than Gold*, August 20, 2001

•*Montana Atlas and Gazette*, Maine, DeLarme, 1997.

•Miller, Preston, "The Fort Connah Restoration Society, *The Bucksin*, 3:3, Big Timber, Dec. 1975.

•Newton, Carl Abbott, A.A., L.L.D., *Montana In The Making,* Gazette Publising Company, 1964.

•Obersinner, Joseph L. S.J., Gritzmacher, Judy, *St. Ignatius Mission: National Historic Site*, Missoula, Gateway, 1977.

•Osburne, Russell, *Journal of a Trapper* 1834-43 (ed. Harris, Aubrey L.) Lincoln, University of Nebraska, 1955.

•Partoll, Albert J. "Fort Connah: A Frontier Trading Post, 1847-1871", *Pacific Northwest Quarterly,* 16, 1925

— "Angus McDonald: Frontier Fur Trader", *Pacific Northwest Quarterly,* 42, 1951.

•Ramsey, Elaine, "The Worth of an Empire, Sir George Simpson Places a Value on the Hudson's Bay Company's American Holdings," *Occurrences, The Journal of Northwest History During the Fur Trade, Spring 2001, Vol. XIX, #2 pp. 9-10*

•Ranft, William Q. "Old-time Christmas Days as Spent on Post Creek", *Western Homeseeker,* 1:3 Missoula: Western Homeseeker, 1905.

•Reinfeld, Fred, Trapppers of The West, Thomas Y. Crowell Company, New York, 1957.

•Ronan, Peter, *History of the Flathead Indians,* Minneapolis, Ross and Haines, 1890.

•Ross, Alexander, *Fur Hunters of The Far West,* University of Oklahoma Press, Norman, Oklahoma, 1956.

•Salish Kootenai College, Catalog, 1999-2001. Pablo, MT. 1999.

•Smiley, H.D. "The Dalliance of David Thompson, *The Beaver*, Winnipeg, Winter, 1972.

•Spritzer, Don, *Roadside History of Montana,* Missoula, Mountain Press, 1999.

•Stone, Arthur L. *Following Old Trails,* Missoula, Pictorial Histories, 1996.

•Terrill, *Black Robe: The Life of Pierre Jean de Smet, Missionary and Pioneer,* New York: Doubleday, 1964.

•Tirrell, Norma, *Montana,* Oakland, Compass American Guides, 1991.

•Tolan, Sister Providencia S.P. *A Shining from the Mountains,* Alberta, Jasper Printing, 1980.

•Watts, Peter, *A Dictionary of the Old West,* 1850-1900, New York, Knopf, 1997.

•Weisel, George F. *Men and Trade on the Northwest Frontier as shown by the Fort Owen Ledger,* Vol. & 2, Bozeman, Montana State University, 1955.

•Wheeler, Keith, *The Chroniclers*, by the Editors of Time-Life Books, New York, 1976.

•Wissler, Clark, *Indians of The United States*, Anchor Books, Doubleday, New York.

LISTING OF BOOKS

Additional copies of **FORT CONNAH,** and many other of Stoneydale Press' books on nature, outdoor recreation, big game hunting, or historical reminisces centered around the Northern Rocky Mountain region, are available at many book stores and sporting goods stores, or direct from Stoneydale Press. If you'd like more information, you can contact us by calling a Toll Free number, **1-800-735-7006,** or by writing the address at the bottom of the page. Here's a partial listing of some of the books that are available:

Historical

Lewis And Clark In The Bitterroot, By The Discovery Writers. Detailed presentation in text, photograph and illustration of the famous Expedition during its two visits to the Bitterroot Mountains in 1805-06. Color section. Hardcover and softcover editions

Lewis and Clark On The Upper Missouri, By The Discovery Writers. Details in text and photograph the Lewis & Clark Expedition on its journey from Fort Mandan along the upper Missouri River to the Continental Divide. Color section. Hardcover and softcover editions.

Dreams Across The Divide: Stories of the Montana Pioneers, Edited by Linda Wostrel, Foreword by Stephen Ambrose. Stories and photos of the first pioneers to settle in Montana. 448 pages, issued in both hardcover and softcover editions..

Montana's Bitterroot Valley, By Russ Lawrence. Big, award winning book of text and color photographs of one of the most scenically stunning areas in America, the Bitterroot valley in western Montana. Many photographs. Softcover

Another Man's Gold: A Novel of the Life & Times of James B. Stuart in Early Montana, By Rod Johnson. Cattle drives, gold panning, rustlers, hangings, battles with outlaws feature this story of one of Montana's first settlers.

Rocky Mountain Spotted Fever in Western Montana: Anatomy of a Pestilence, By Dr. Robert N. Philip. This book details the triumph of medical science over the pestilence of Rocky Mountain Spotted Fever by chronicling the efforts of the U.S. Public Health Service. A wonderful historical account of this stupendous achievement. 206 pages, 6x9-inch softcover format.

Indian Trails of The Northern Rockies, By Darris Flanagan. A detailed, precisely-written look at the significant trails and mountain passes used by the Kutenai Indians of northwestern Montana and British Columbia to access the buffalo country on the high plains to the east. Plus stories of subsequent use and change. Softcover.

The Elk Mystique, By Mike Lapinski, large format, magnificently beautiful all-color presentation in photo and text of the story of the wapiti, the American elk. Softcover, 144 pages.

STONEYDALE PRESS PUBLISHING COMPANY
523 Main Street • Box 188
Stevensville, Montana 59870
Phone: 406-777-2729